MAVERICK LEADERSHIP

For real estate
Fernando is #1

MAVERICK LEADERSHIP

PRACTICAL ADVICE FOR GENERAL MANAGERS, ENTREPRENEURS & CEOs

HUGH LATIF

New Covenant Canada Book

New Covenant Canada Book
Division of 1008230 Ontario Ltd.

Library and Archives Canada Cataloguing in Publication information available upon request.
ISBN: 978-0-9950732-0-3

New Covenant Canada Book
Hugh Latif & Associates Management Consultants
Deloitte Building
400 Applewood Cresent, Suite 100
Vaughan, Ontario, L4K 0C3 Canada

hughlatif.com

Cover and text design: Tania Craan
Cover photograph: monaelisaphoto.com
Copy edit: Jen Knoch
Electronic formatting: Troy Cunningham

Printed and bound in Canada

TABLE OF CONTENTS

INTRODUCTION

Initially, *Maverick Leadership*© came out of my newsletter *Marketing Instinct*©, which consisted of 15 issues published through my consulting company. I always received favorable comments from clients about the content of my newsletter, and thought it would be good to have these comments reprinted in a booklet format and then used as a hand-out to both current and prospective clients.

But, after reviewing the material, and meeting with my dear friend and associate Priya Devalia, I was convinced that a book that would group together all the useful information contained in these newsletters was a viable pursuit.

I began to expand on my topics and write brand new chapters with fresh insights that held time-honored, tried and tested methods. As I mined my 40-plus years of business experience, I realized that gathering together and writing all this practical business information would be of tremendous help to young general managers, entrepreneurs and CEOs. And that's how *Maverick Leadership*© was born!

Maverick Leadership© contains practical advice on key subjects about management. My objective is to provide practical help to general managers, entrepreneurs and CEOs, and give them proven advice for their daily job.

Successful management depends on strong leadership and business acumen, but there are many small, significant things that are not covered by business courses taught at universities and colleges.

Maverick Leadership© is like a personal mentor giving the reader practical advice and guidance, specific suggestions and recommendations that have worked for me and that have produced powerful results. The information is not academic, but it takes its cue from the frontline of day-to-day management.

My first career of 21 years with the Dun & Bradstreet Nielsen Group gave me the discipline of working for a large global company. Since I worked in several countries including Canada, Italy, Brazil and France, the reader will find the experience I have gained will be applicable across different cultures and business environments, especially for North and South America, and Europe.

In my second career, over the past 20 years, I have been a management consultant to small- and medium-size Canadian businesses that are privately owned and family run. During this time I conducted over 300 consulting assignments that included business turnarounds, succession planning, strategic planning and the set-up and launch of advisory boards.

Maverick Leadership© tries to incorporate all the knowledge and experience from these consulting mandates with incredible insights into what works and what doesn't. These assignments included manufacturers, distributors, business services, retailers and other industries. In short, they cover a wide spectrum of business activities.

Management is taught in business schools, but the academic part does not guarantee success. It is only the practical day-to-day experience that makes good general managers (GMs). This book is about practical advice, down-to-earth do's and don'ts and proven ways to manage.

Maverick Leadership© is a manual on the key elements of good management, and on GM duties and responsibilities. It should be considered a good training manual and reference book for everyday management.

Of all the skills and traits we will discuss in *Maverick Leadership*©, **strong leadership and team-building** are the two most important keys to business success.

While many of the suggestions and tips contained in *Maverick*

Leadership© may not be new, I believe my presentation is friendly and straightforward. It is ready to use and easy to access, and readers will be able to understand the keys to business success. And all this in one reference manual!

Finally, the book is organized so the reader can easily go back and forth, and select a certain subject for re-reading and reference purposes. Each chapter contains my experience with a specific subject: strategy, HR selection and recruitment, advisory boards, pricing of products/services, to name a few.

As for the style and tone of *Maverick Leadership©*, I have worked hard to keep the language simple and straightforward. I wanted to maintain a conversational tone so you, the reader, and I are in an informal setting. It would be like two business professionals enjoying a cup of coffee or tea, while obtaining counsel on a subject or situation happening in your business. In this way you have two friends sharing experiences, but one is older with more business experience.

I describe *Maverick Leadership©* as "practical" because that's what characterizes all my business practices. They must be practical things that can make a difference through daily use and application, followed by real results.

How good is the advice contained in *Maverick Leadership©*? That is a good question!

The purpose of this book is not to self promote, but to share the proven strategies and tactics I have learned, and to encourage a new wave of business leaders.

I had two incredibly successful careers in the corporate world, and in building businesses from a wide array of sectors. I have been consistently blessed with exceptional teams working under me and alongside me.

Great people who worked for me also excelled in their subsequent careers. Over the years and across the oceans, I have kept in touch with many of my senior managers, many of whom are now successful presidents, CEOs and senior executives of public and private companies. I can't guarantee that following my suggestions will make you 100% successful, but *Maverick Leadership©* will help you make a significant improvement to your managerial skills, and that will result in better business outcomes.

In my first career, when I got to **Italy** in 1981, the Italian company I was working with had lost $1.8M on sales of $6M! Six years later when I left, sales were $65M with a bottom line of $15M. For sure, acquisitions contributed to these results, but the acquisitions were made to accelerate our success. In those six years we went from being the last country unit on a performance list of 28 international companies of the D&B GROUP to number 2.

In **Brazil** the company I was working with had sales of $12M and a small bottom line. Two years later, we had increased sales by 50% and profits by over 600%. When I arrived in **France**, the French business unit I was with had been operating in the red for seven straight years. Thanks to a fantastic team, we got the company to operate in the black within six months, and three years later we had increased sales by 30% and achieved an operating margin of more than 25%.

I returned to **Canada** with Nielsen in 1992, and for the first time my assignment was not a turnaround. The Canadian company was profitable, and the local market leader. However, results were flat and the company was under serious attack from its largest US competitor. In just over four years, we turned stagnation into a rapidly growing, vibrant company where sales went from $65M to $95M. The company was robust and healthy with an enviable bottom line. We also put in place a moat around the business that has kept competitors at bay to this day!

Strategy is not only about achieving growth, but about building sustainable healthy businesses. I look back at some strategic moats we built from 1992 to 1996 and can't help but smile when I realize that, 20 years later, these moats are still keeping competitors on the defensive.

I am not mentioning these results simply to boast. What I want readers to focus on is this: the advice and suggestions contained in *Maverick Leadership©* stand on concrete and measurable business results.

My experience is diversified, deep and rich. With *Maverick Leadership©* I have tried to include what works and what doesn't, along with how to set priorities, how to differentiate between the urgent and the important and, finally, how to make decisions and deal with difficult situations.

Maverick Leadership© is a great resource for people who seek self-development, look to be promoted or just want insights and proven methods that can be applied rapidly and effectively.

I was recently asked about the top three things that contribute to personal, professional and business success. While I was tempted to give a long list of things contained in *Maverick Leadership*©, here are my top three favorites:

The first thing is to work in your area of **passion**. You must have passion for the business you are in. This cannot be taught and learned. I am a good consultant because I have a passion for consulting. Don't work outside your area of passion.

The second thing is **integrity** and strong ethics. Leading people effectively depends on trust, and if you can be trusted, you will be a good leader. You can't lead people who don't trust you. An officer may have authority over his or her soldiers, but a strong leader and not just an officer requires trust.

Lastly, a successful leader must be able to not only change but embrace **change**. Today's business environment is constantly changing — and rapidly. Success requires the ability to change, to be flexible, to innovate and to constantly seek new ways of serving customers.

I may oversimplify things, and that can be both a strength and a weakness. But it is this straightforward and easily accessible simplicity that encapsulates the practical nature of this book. However, I truly believe that having a passion for the business, high integrity and the ability to embrace change are the top three ingredients for success.

So grab yourself a cup of coffee or tea and let's sit down for a *Maverick Leadership*© chat. I hope and trust *Maverick Leadership*© will become a close companion and coach for you.

My best sincere wishes for success,
Hugh Latif

CHAPTER 1

NAVIGATING SUCCESSFULLY THROUGH THE STAGES OF GROWTH

"The goal as a company is to have customer service that is not just the best but legendary."
— Sam Walton

Making a difference

Making a difference and achieving success as a general manager (GM), CEO or entrepreneur does not depend on set formulas, intellectual know-how and/or academic knowledge. You cannot just take ready-made business recipes and apply them, which is often the perception with how-to books and business articles on the "Top Ten Steps" to success in this or that.

A combination of complex factors must come together to be translated into success. Absence of one or more of these required factors can be a real hindrance to success.

Some important attributes of a good CEO are a vigorous flair for business, strong management skills, leadership traits, financial capabilities, innovative talents, ethical behavior, decision-making abilities, good timing and planning skills. These, and many more characteristics, are all key components for successful business management.

The six stages of growth

However, the greatest of all these elements is the ability of the entrepreneur, owner or CEO to skillfully take the organization through the various stages of growth.

Neil C. Churchill and Virginia L. Lewis, in their *HBR* article "The Five Stages of Small Business Growth," list the following five stages: Existence, Survival, Success, Take-off and Resource Maturity.[1] Sue Hansen, on the other hand, pinpoints seven stages of business growth: Start Up, Ramp Up, Delegation, Professional, Integration, Strategic and Visionary.[2]

A survey conducted by Statistics Canada for the CEOs of leading growth firms in Ontario identified six distinct stages of enterprise growth as follows: Stage 1 — One-Person Bands, Stage 2 — Early Success, Stage 3 — Operationalizing, Stage 4 — The People Crunch, Stage 5 — Professionalizing, Stage 6 – The Corporation.[3]

Whether there are five, six or seven stages of growth is not important. It is more important for entrepreneurs to know that they must shift gears as they grow their companies, and recognize that to achieve growth and success they need to move swiftly between the various stages of growth.

While each stage has its own characteristics and challenges, the bottom line is: How can CEOs adapt through the various roles required of them? How do they move from the role of doing to supervising, and then from managing to ultimately leading? How do entrepreneurs, owners or CEOs graduate from the school of "If you want it done right, do it yourself"? How do they move from being the lead violinist (an instrumental player) to the orchestra conductor?

---

1 Neil C. Churchill and Virginia L. Lewis, "The Five Stages of Small Business Growth," *hbr.org*, May 1983, https://hbr.org/1983/05/the-five-stages-of-small-business-growth, (accessed April 23, 2015).

2 Sue Hansen, "7 Stages of Business Growth Review," *suehansenspeaks.com*, http://www.suehansenspeaks.com/business/stages.htm (accessed April 23, 2015).

3 Donald Rumball, "The Six Stages of Growth in Ontario's Leading Growth Firms," *Ontario.ca*, March 2013, http://www.ontario.ca/document/six-stages-growth-ontarios-leading-growth-firms (accessed April 23, 2015), 8, 10, 13, 16, 19, 23, 26.

Most often, business academia relates this to the skill of being able to delegate. While delegating is important, there is a need to go beyond delegating. Here are key points to consider:

- Entrusting people with parts of the business
- Taking delegation to a higher level where the CEO functions as guide and coach, allowing team members to take the ball and run with it
- Learning how to accept mistakes and errors
- Learning how to deal with mistakes and errors in a constructive manner that develops team members rather than destroying their confidence
- Putting together a strong team whose members work well together, complement each other and above all are committed to the overall goals of the organization

This is a very powerful list of key skills. Take a moment and think about each of the five points mentioned. Do you trust people? Are you a good coach? Can you become a good coach? Do you like being a coach? How do you react when members of your team make errors? Take every point and self-evaluate or rate yourself as to how it applies to you as a manager.

Can the CEO trust others? Does the CEO have an eye for selecting capable team members who have potential for advancement? Can the CEO develop their team members' skills both individually and as part of a team? These and other questions help reveal the current stage of the company's evolution and whether or not the CEO can successfully take the organization to the next level.

I have seen many organizations where the entrepreneur/owner or CEO has created a situation where almost everyone reports to him or her. The organizational chart is horizontal, and as new members join the team, they all report to that one boss who is the owner or CEO.

Others have a more traditional organization with neat boxes and fancy titles that give the illusion that there is a chain of command. However, all decisions are still centralized at the CEO level. These CEOs often work 60-plus hours per week. They run the risk of burnout, and can no longer keep an eye on the big picture and the destiny of the company. Direction and strategic energy are lost in cases like these.

CEO character and personality are key

It is crucial to take the character and personality of the CEO into account, as well as their management and leadership style. You will find that in virtually all cases when you consult or examine an organization's CEO, that person is unable to change their leadership style even though he or she wants to change it.

In some cases, CEOs have the ability to change their style, but do not want to change. The ability or willingness of CEOs to alter their leadership style is significant because it applies to succession issues where the owner is a parent handing the baton to a child.

A Grant Thornton LLP survey revealed that 70% of family-owned businesses do not pass on the reins of a company to a second generation.[4] And only one out of ten businesses moves into the hands of a third generation. This clearly demonstrates the need for greater succession planning and for executive coaching, as well as mentoring and skill development initiatives.

Identifying the winning strategy is the easier part of the two components. However, it is in implementation or execution where real leadership and management abilities are demonstrated.

Many would say that entrepreneurs do not make good managers and good managers do not make good entrepreneurs. While this is true in many cases, it is an oversimplification. It is important to keep focus on solutions that do not just treat the symptoms of the problem, but that provide for healthy and durable solutions.

If the entrepreneur is not a good manager, they require coaching in order to develop their skills or to work on reinforcing the team with strong managers who will compensate for this shortcoming. The key is to address the real hindrances with practical solutions that make the difference you're looking for.

---

4 Grant Thornton LLP, "Private Company Succession Planning: Where do you stand?" *grantthornton.ca*, 2011, http://www.grantthornton.ca/resources/insights/reports/Private_Company_Sucession_Planning_Where_do_you_stand_2011.pdf (accessed April 23, 2015), 12–16.

Doing more is not the answer

As the business grows, more delegation is required along with more planning. The source of the advice cannot come only from the customer with access to more capital becoming a priority.

In their early career most entrepreneurs think the best advice comes from their existing customers, and that all they need is more money to grow the business. While customers' advice and having adequate capital are both important, this is an oversimplification.

At some stage in the life of a company, relying exclusively on customer advice is not ideal. You need to seek more in-depth research and advice from experts who have exposure, experience and know-how. It's the same with money. If money could solve all problems, why do big companies fail? Large corporations have access to capital, yet they still have the potential to fail. Doing more is not the answer. It is doing a specific set of correct actions that results in success.

A more formal organizational structure must be created where management depth is needed. At this point of growth, seeking external expertise is crucial.

Many CEOs think that doing more of what they have done in the past will suffice, however, this is not true. A CEO must change with the situation and evolve with the requirements needed to keep moving forward, not backwards.

There are three key issues that CEOs should maintain as real objectives to driving successful growth:

1) Shaping the performance of the business and delivering results
2) Developing a strategy that continuously adapts to changing market conditions
3) Managing their organization talent: selecting, retaining, developing, managing and leading a strong team

Here is a brief explanation of all three key objectives:

1) Shaping the performance of the business means having set objectives and targets.

These should include financial targets (e.g., sales and revenues, gross profits, margins, costs, return on equity, return on assets, financial ratios, etc.). Measuring productivity, quality, customer satisfaction, new business, repeat business, inventory levels and accounts-receivable collection performance are all examples of key objectives that demonstrate how good a business is overall.

It is not sufficient to claim that you have all the data inside your head and you understand it intrinsically. Financial and operational measurements must translate into the business performance of the organization, and must be put in writing.

When these measurements are clear in black and white, they raise the level of accountability for the people involved. They help prevent making excuses, and serve as the dividing lines that show each performance grade. When compared year over year or quarter over quarter, they also show business trends for productivity and for processes with leadership decision-making. It is vital that a CEO continues to ascertain whether the organization is improving or headed for failure.

I cannot overemphasize the importance of having clear and measurable objectives. I am sure you must have heard of the saying "If you do not know where you are going, you will never know if you are lost!" Another common quote is "What gets measured gets managed."

Many organizations rely on doing better than last year. Their intra-organizational dialogue says, "If we did $10M in sales last year, then we should beat this number by selling more this year," and so on. That is not objective setting.

Objective setting must be recalculated in terms of reviewing the key objectives of the organization, evaluating the opportunities and challenges of the marketplace and assessing your resources and all the factors that influence your performance. Then you should set a new objective for the organization, along with the team that will be responsible for achieving the objective.

and flexible. They need to constantly put their strategies to the test and update them. They need to continually attract and develop human talent, and then put together strong teams that are able to execute. Later in this book, I will explain how to navigate successfully through the various stages of growth.

CHAPTER 2

SMALL IS BEAUTIFUL

Strategies for Sustaining Profitable, Healthy Growth

"Do what you do so well that they will want to see it again and bring their friends."
— Walt Disney

Business is operating today in a market that is evolving at an unprecedented speed. Almost every industry and sector of the economy is experiencing rapid change. Profound changes are happening at the macro and micro levels.

Consider the following **macro trends**: **International trade** is on the rise and the flow of free trade is steadily increasing. **Cross-border investments** are on the increase and the movement of capital is largely unrestricted. **Consumer preferences** and shopping habits have changed through the big box retailers, e-commerce and the Internet. **Savings rates** continue to experience massive shifts.

The **financial markets**, after sustaining incredible growth, have lost remarkable ground during the past few years, but have bounced back and continue to experience changes. And, of course, **technology** is advancing at the speed of light with no visible sign of slowing down. Thus, tremendous change is happening at the macro level.

Now let's take a look at **micro trends** that are specific to the business environment: Large, well-established businesses that should withstand any storm are failing miserably. Whether they operate in the mature old economy or the new economy does not seem to make any difference. It has no bearing on whether they are department stores, music retailers, airlines, auto manufacturers, high-tech or Internet start-ups. Some have gone, many are bleeding and several appear to be slowly but surely on their way to the graveyard.

The term "big corporation" was once synonymous with strength and invulnerability. After all, these corporations attract the best talent, have access to capital, can afford expert advice and use the latest technology. So why do they fail?

Research in North America reveals that the average corporation loses half of its customers within five years, 50% of its employees within four years and half of its investors in one single year.[1] Newer research says that companies now lose anywhere from 20% to 50% of their employees in just one year.[2] These are staggering numbers.

Fast **customer turnover** is due to the lack of customer focus by your average large corporation. While large corporations speak about customer focus and customer care, they constantly fail to get it right. Unmotivated frontline workers, and inattentive and impersonal service become the norm.

Call centers that are supposed to provide good service are instead providing slow, impersonal and incompetent service. In fact, some call centers even give the impression that they are designed to do the opposite, and actually discourage customer calls.

In addressing **employee turnover**, large corporations have placed a low importance on loyalty to their employees. The fallout is that employees, in turn, don't see any benefit in maintaining a sense of loyalty to the corporation.

Massive layoffs appear to be made without even minimal regret and without any hesitation whatsoever. At the same time, executive pay is higher than ever. One of the largest business losses ever recorded in

---

1 Anders Gronstedt, *The Customer Century: Lessons from World Class Companies in Integrated Communications* (New York: Routledge, 2000), 290.

2 Wharton University of Pennsylvania, "Declining Employee Loyalty: A Casualty of the New Workplace," May 9, 2012, http://knowledge.wharton.upenn.edu/article/declining-employee-loyalty-a-casualty-of-the-new-workplace/ (accessed April 23, 2015).

North America was sustained by a big company which, during the same year as that loss, had three executives make the list of the top five highest-paid executives in the country. It would be difficult to ask an employee to have professional and ethical respect for their management team or for the board of directors which authorized such a payout.

It is no wonder investors, including large institutional ones, have very little loyalty to their portfolio of investments. Stocks are bought and dumped with no hesitation. Greed has made its way to the top of large business in North America.

So, while large business has access to considerable resources and should be well-positioned to prosper, we now see that the factors which represent opportunities (e.g., technology, competitive marketplace and changing customer needs) are the very same factors that expose management mediocrity as never before.

At the executive and board levels, decisions appear to be made without any regard for strategy, with no accountability, and with little regard for the human resources factor of a company. And HR is the most important engine for success or failure.

This may surprise you, but in today's fast-paced marketplace, I believe that small and medium-size businesses have a definitive competitive edge.

Here is why:

- **Team Play:** A smaller team with focus, determination and higher motivation is indeed more powerful than a large corporation run by remote control from an ivory tower. The corporation may look impressive because of its size, but once you start digging, you find teams are impotent because they are nameless and feel indispensable within the large corporate machine.

  A small but determined and well-motivated team can accomplish just as much as a huge roster of employees who are demoralized through management neglect. That's how a soccer team can win against an "all-star team" — the players know each other well and play as a team rather than as a group of famous players with big egos who are stars individually but have no team spirit.

- **Real Customer Focus:** A smaller company has closer contact with its customer base, and a clearer understanding of what those customers like and dislike. They know what excites a customer, what their price tolerance is and what alternative choices might appeal to them.

  CEOs who stay close to customers make better decisions than CEOs who spend most of their time in boardrooms. I always coach my clients as follows: "Don't live on the frontline, but be comfortable on the frontline and know what is happening on the frontline."
- **Technology Use:** A smaller company can use technology effectively and leapfrog over a big corporation to get the business. Small-sized organizations do not have to go through a long evolutionary cycle since technology allows them to accelerate the stages of growth. Of course, this involves a certain measure of risk, but the opportunity to bypass a long growth cycle is far more doable now than anytime before.

  Technology today is available at lower costs. This can help make small and medium-size businesses improve their position by accelerating past or moving alongside large corporations quickly by skipping some stages or growth process. Just look at what is available through cloud computing and the Internet. You get top-notch services and tools for a fraction of what they cost a few years ago.
- **Lower Overhead:** Small businesses have lower overhead and can pass on cost advantages to their customers without sacrificing profitability. No ridiculous compensation packages exist at the top, and there is no layer upon layer of ineffective management. Incentives are deployed toward the employees themselves, and team morale and teamwork are at a high level. There are also no big unions that kill innovation and promote the status quo in a small corporation.

  Just think about Avis, the large car rental company, which acquired Zipcar in 2013 for $500M.[3] Zipcar had a 9,000 car fleet vs. Avis' fleet of 500,000. Zipcar had a handful of employees vs. Avis' 26,000 employees.

---

3 Guy Dixon, "Avis overcomes reservations with purchase of Zipcar," *Globe and Mail*, January 2, 2013 (accessed April 23, 2015).

- **Speed:** Small and mid-size businesses can be more flexible and agile in adapting to market conditions. They can capture opportunities and change course much more quickly than large players. This agility, due to their smaller size, gives them an unexpected edge over large, cumbersome counterparts that are slow to make changes.

These factors, however, do not automatically spell success for small businesses. But when recognized, they can translate into opportunities and be used to their advantage. As a small/medium-size business, you also have limitations and forces that are working against you. As a management consultant to small and medium-size businesses, my experience over the last 20 years has shown me the pitfalls of small business.

How you can avoid these pitfalls:

Strategic planning

Small businesses seldom prepare a strategic plan and this is a big mistake. Make sure you put together a good strategy. Do not just make a budget, but also make long-term plans. Engage with your team and formulate a strategy for the next few years. It does not have to be an elaborate document, but it should be clear and precise, and have strategic intelligence. Strategic planning clarifies where you are, where you are going and what needs to be done to get you there.

Spelling out your vision for the business is essential. Without a clearly communicated vision, the business will not be able to survive. Leadership at the top of the organizational structure needs to be equipped with viable tools that give them the skill, passion and ability to impart this vision to those they are leading. It is not enough for only those at the top to understand the vision. For the organization to thrive, every employee at every level must understand the vision.

Insights into market, customers and prospects

Do your homework on the marketplace frequently and find out the answers to important questions such as:

- What are the driving forces in the marketplace?
- What changes have occurred and what are the consequences?
- Have customers' preferences changed?
- How are these changes affecting your sales and marketing activities?
- How is your repeat business?
- Do customers come back and why?
- Do they go elsewhere and why?
- Are there any other needs that are not met by your line of products/services?
- How is your new business?
- Is your customer base growing or is it declining in numbers, and if so, why?
- Are you fishing in the same old customer pool or are you finding new customer sources?
- Are you fishing for the same traditional customers or are you finding new types of customers?
- How are your sales costs performing as a percentage of sales?

Find out what's happening with the marketplace and in your specific industry. Answering all these questions will help you adjust accordingly and maintain your strategic integrity.

Competitive intelligence

Keep checking on your competition and discovering how you can keep your competitive edge sharper than theirs. Do you know what the competition is up to? Where do they aim to go? Wayne Gretzky once said: "A good hockey player plays where the puck is. A great hockey player plays where the puck is going to be."

Some good questions to ask about competitive intelligence gathering are:

- What are their prices and when were they last changed?
- What will they most likely do in the future?
- Are there newcomers in your marketplace?
- Have any competitors left the market?
- Are there any changes of ownership or any changes in management ranks?
- Do you periodically visit your competitors' websites? What's new?
- How does your website compare with the others?
- When you use search engines, does your website come up in the first 10, 20 or 30 search options?

Check out your competitors periodically and systematically, and maintain your aura of being a viable threat that is fully aware of their plans, products and strategies.

Competitive intelligence information is usually assembled by the sales force, but that should not be the only source of information. You should also use your own customers, prospects, suppliers, associations, Internet research, media, credit reports and market studies. At least once a year you should conduct a thorough review of the competitive landscape of your business. Lastly, you should also use third-party research to complement your own team's work in this area to ensure that the information is coming from unbiased sources.

Some experts say it is better to concentrate on doing things right, and focus on your own products and services rather than focus on that of your competitors. Ultimately, you can only influence change on your side, but not on theirs. While this is true, and I don't disagree, I still believe that doing more research on your competitors is key to your success for three main reasons:

1) Knowing what the competition is up to allows you to better respond rather than react after the fact.
2) Doing your homework on the competition allows you to identify their weaknesses and then use the areas of weakness to your advantage.

3) Because competitors offer an alternative choice to the customer, it is good to know where the tilting point is so you can better satisfy customer needs. Influencing the tilting point to your advantage makes it harder for your competitors to steal your customers.

Financial and operational objectives

Most businesspeople look closely at their profit-and-loss statement. They attempt to keep their profitability under check, and they should. But do you also look at your balance sheet? Do you review your capitalization? Do you assess your debt-to-worth ratio? What about your working capital requirements?

Get more people to look at these financials. Don't limit the scrutiny of these elements to the CFO. More eyes on the bottom line result in an overall improvement of the bottom line itself.

Financial figures aside, do you also set objectives for the various parts of your business? Is productivity measured? Is quality tracked? Does your team have monthly and quarterly objectives? Do you set standards of performance? All these actions can make a big difference. Remember Peter Drucker's famous quote: "What gets measured, gets managed."

Back to basics, receivables and inventory

In most businesses, accounts receivable and inventory represent the largest portion of the total assets of the business. Still, for most small and medium-size businesses, no specific people are accountable for watching over these two types of assets. Usually, slow collections are caused by the lack of consistent follow-up, and the lack of disciplined billing and collection procedures. Slow-turning inventory is often caused by the lack of inventory management, rather than just being an indication of sales performance. Making one person accountable for credit controls, receivables collection and turnover and another person responsible for inventory control and management can make a big difference to your operating results and balance sheet.

While these two assets (accounts receivable and inventory) will ultimately report to the financial manager, a specific person should be in charge of accounts receivable. A credit-and-collection policy should be established and followed and a clear and precise process put in place for collection of receivables. Salespeople can help in the collection or complement your process, but someone like the credit manager or A/R clerk should be responsible.

This is also the same for inventory — a specific person must be in charge of inventory alone. Again, the salespeople will influence and complement how inventory is managed, but a specific person must be given the responsibility of managing inventory (levels, categories, items, size, turnover, etc.).

I have found that slow receivables are not always the result of slow-paying customers. Time and time again I find that slow receivables are usually the result of my client not following up on their own receivables. If you do not have a disciplined process to speed up collection, your customers will take advantage of that and pay you slowly. There is a saying in the trade: "The wheel that squeaks gets the grease!"

Similarly for inventory, for one client we classified products into A, B, C and D items. The A items were products that were in high demand and turned quickly, the B items were the next category, and so on with C and D items. We found out that A items represented 10% of total products, but accounted for 45% of sales. B products represented 15% of products but accounted for 30% of sales. Managing items A and B more closely (they represented 25% of total products and 75% of sales), allowed the company to improve service and reduce its overall investment in inventory.

Managing receivables and inventory levels is not rocket science. What it really needs is focus, consistency and accountability. I am sure Amazon and Caterpillar would have a more complex inventory-management system, but what I am recommending for most businesses will provide so much benefit on both sides: to customer service, and a vitamin shot to your working capital!

Human resources and organizational structure

An organizational structure must evolve with the business. Ask yourself:

- Is your organization in a start-up phase, growth phase or mature phase?
- Are you targeting rapid sales growth or are you focusing on bottom-line improvements?
- Are you attacking, defending, consolidating or doing something else?
- Is your focus on sales or marketing?
- Are production and operations the key drivers or are the sales and marketing functions the key drivers?

All these different criteria have a big impact on how you organize your business.

While the organizational structure must have some stability, it cannot be written in stone to the point of being inflexible. But it does become that way when ego and protecting turf take over.

The business issues (opportunities, challenges, strategies, etc.) must drive the organizational structure, not the other way around. Of course, good managers must also take into account the calibre of people at their disposal. However, this may be satisfactory for the short-term, but not for the long-term. If you need new talent or specific skills to maintain organizational health, then you must get them. Procrastination in getting talent with the required skill set will only prolong the ill health of your company.

For those who are soccer fans, soccer coaches constantly change the positioning of players on their team. This depends on such elements as the availability of players, as well as strategy, tactics and the opponent. You will see players with a formation of 4-3-3 or 4-4-2 or 4-5-1, as the situation warrants.

Getting a tune-up

Do you think it is a good idea to visit the car dealer once a year for a check-up, even when you have absolutely no problem with your automobile? The answer is yes. The cost of maintenance is generally much lower than the cost of fixing. How does this apply to business?

As you make decisions and plan your strategies, it is good to take counsel from trusted advisors. This may sound like a self-serving statement from a management consultant. But the truth is a variety of opinions tends to bring safety and ensure success. As your business grows, it will go through stages of transitions. These transitions tend to be filled with tension, uncertainty and doubt. It takes careful planning for things to go right during those stages of growth.

So expose your business to a frequent check-up by an external party who is independent, knowledgeable and trustworthy. Seek advice and counsel.

Good independent business counsel can bring objectivity to your decision-making, and external expertise can bring knowledge to your planning process. A trustworthy consultant or a full advisory board may be able to provide this tune-up. This way you can capture all the opportunities presented for a small business and avoid the pitfalls of being small. In the long run, doing these things will help you progress from being small to being big. See the advisory board chapter for more information on how an advisory board can bring competitive advantage to your organization.

CHAPTER 3

STRATEGIC PLANNING

Short Term vs. Long Term
The Necessity of Driving with a Road Map

"However beautiful the strategy,
you should occasionally look at the results."
— Winston Churchill

You could be at the wheel of a beautiful red Ferrari, but going in the wrong direction. Do you think you would get to your destination? The answer is obviously no. This is what happens when companies don't have a road map that clearly lays out a successful, efficient path to their destination. This road map is called a strategic plan.

If you're doing well in your business, you want to put in place a plan to stay on course. If you're facing obstacles, you want to know why. Are your problems momentary or a trend? Is there an industry-wide symptom? Is your strategy correct or is its execution faulty? Is the execution of the strategy at fault or is the leadership weak?

Let us first clear up a misconception among business owners and entrepreneurs who think strategic planning is best left to large companies and corporations. A strategic plan is really the process of developing and maintaining a viable fit among your company objectives, resources and market opportunities.

Your plan doesn't have to be a huge document. In fact, the content of a strategic plan depends on the size and complexity of your company.

A strategic plan is often confused with a business plan. Let me clarify the difference between the two.

A strategic plan is your overall "big picture" plan. Under such a plan, you may have several business plans addressing specific aspects and issues such as specific product lines, services, geography, human resources, financial issues, operations details and other components.

So what can small and medium-sized businesses expect to see in a strategic plan?

Simply put, you want to spell out **where you are today, where you want to be tomorrow, and how you will get there**.

A strategic plan usually includes a good description of the marketplace and the dynamics of the market, as well as what is changing in the landscape and how these changes translate for you in terms of opportunities or threats. Most importantly, it contains how you will respond to these changes.

A strategic plan also includes SWOT analysis of your company (Strengths, Weaknesses, Opportunities, Threats). You also usually find a section on the competitive landscape, along with a description and analysis of your competitors and those who may become competitors in the future.

A good strategic plan also includes key strategies to achieve your objectives. Strategies are different from tactics. Here is the difference. A strategy calling for geographical growth may involve several tactical actions to support that strategy. For example, this may include opening a new branch in a city not covered by you before, hiring a new manager and staff, joining forces with a local player or acquiring a potential competitor. All these can be described as tactical moves to achieve the strategic objective of geographical expansion. These are the standard sections you find in most strategic plans. My favorite parts, though, are the following:

Organizational structure

One of the first topics on my list is a company's organizational structure. Traditionally, the structure of your organization evolves historically, which might be akin to adding seats to the bus as you need them. But at some point you need to know where you're going and if you need a bigger bus.

Typically, entrepreneurs may have everybody in the company reporting to the president/owner, but what is needed for future growth of the company is structuring the company so you can delegate strategy. You want senior people to help you bring the strategy from the top, and then integrate it throughout the ranks of the company.

How you organize your team is key to executing your strategy with excellence. For example, if the strategy is to expand globally, you need to consider what kind of organizational structure will help you achieve that goal. If your strategy calls for growth by acquisition, then your organizational structure must be responsive to this type of strategy, and so on.

People resources

A strategic plan also addresses important aspects of the business such as human resources. You may need new talent but feel that you can't afford it. However, you don't have to buy the cinema just to see a movie. Many entrepreneurs fail to realize that they can build their teams with outside consultants and get their expertise without full-time hiring. Companies can also build alliances and strategic partnerships to reinforce their existing resources. This allows you to expand and penetrate new markets, and to share the risk involved.

Critical success factors

Along with having the right human resources in place, a good plan also includes critical success factors, which are essential elements you need to get where you want to go. Most people instinctively know where they want to go. It's how to get there that is the challenge.

A strategic plan allows companies to map out their tactics one step at a time. It won't be a straight line. You have to think progressively and establish milestones toward your destination. In a strategic plan you need strong leadership as a critical success factor. This is strong leadership that can take charge and stick to a strategic plan, while building buy-in and team involvement.

Another important priority is having an outside facilitator or advisor involved in strategic planning. This can take away some of the pressure. An outside source gives you an objective viewpoint, helps you resolve conflict and ensures that your people respect their goals and commitments. I recommend that entrepreneurs make good use of specialized experts who have in-depth knowledge of strategic planning.

Investments and capital requirements

If you're pumping water more slowly than the tap is filling your bathtub, eventually you'll be in trouble. What does this have to do with strategic planning? Strategic planning also deals with ways of maintaining capital in your company, whether it's used for buying equipment or simply keeping money in the bank for tough times. What's vital today is being innovative with your financing and applying some outside-the-box thinking.

Most entrepreneurs focus only on the cost of money, which is expressed in the rate of interest they pay. They fail to realize that an interest rate is not the only thing to assess in your bank/financier relationship. You have to look at the overall relationship and how you're benefiting from it in the long term.

Occasionally, you can get caught with rapid growth, which creates a situation of tight working capital with the occasional cash-flow bottlenecks. This should be fixed quickly. Being undercapitalized is like having a small gasoline tank in your car; frequent stops to refuel will affect your speed, so even when driving a Ferrari, you will be handicapped by the stops to refuel and lose the race. Make sure you are well-capitalized for the job ahead.

Objectives and rewards

Strategies and tactics aside, I think the performance of employees is a make or break factor for success. Naturally, you should reward them so they remain loyal to your company. You have to ignite in people a real desire to get the job done. A sound strategic plan outlines your reward tactics, whether it's putting bonuses in place or simply maintaining ongoing, open communications with employees. Entrepreneurs should also consider rewarding employees for strategic wins such as penetrating a new market or gaining a new strategic customer.

Timing, priorities and tracking

Being realistic about expectations and making goals attainable are also integral parts of strategic planning. Employees have to understand your priorities, whether it's building your customer base or increasing revenues, focusing on market share or R&D, acquiring new clients or improving the margin.

I give these examples not to imply that you should choose to do one or the other, but to underline the need to have your whole team focused on the right objectives. This way team members know what the overall goal is and work effectively together. Too often I see employees stuck in invisible silos with individual objectives that don't do a good job of contributing to the overall corporate objectives.

Once your objectives are in place, it's also important to plan how you'll report and track performance. Although entrepreneurs may assume that a good monitoring system is basically a financial statement, I believe that tracking and reporting goes much further than this. You should be sure that you have information on productivity and quality achievements, and forecasts that let you see clearly where you are heading. For more information on this important subject, review the KPI (Key Performance Indicators) chapter.

Competitive arena

Most small and medium-sized businesses do an assessment of their competitive market before getting started, and then rely on informal updates and feedback from the sales force. But precious few do the proper follow-up and engage in the discipline of providing an update. You have to make this assessment an ongoing process in the company. Check competitors frequently, systematically and as thoroughly as you can. This is not only to defend yourself, but to design tactics that allow you to benefit from their weaknesses.

Strategic planning is a vital tool for entrepreneurs today, no matter the size of the business. A strategic plan that is well thought out, well executed, well maintained and up to date can put you on the best route for improved business performance.

The strategic planning process in a nutshell

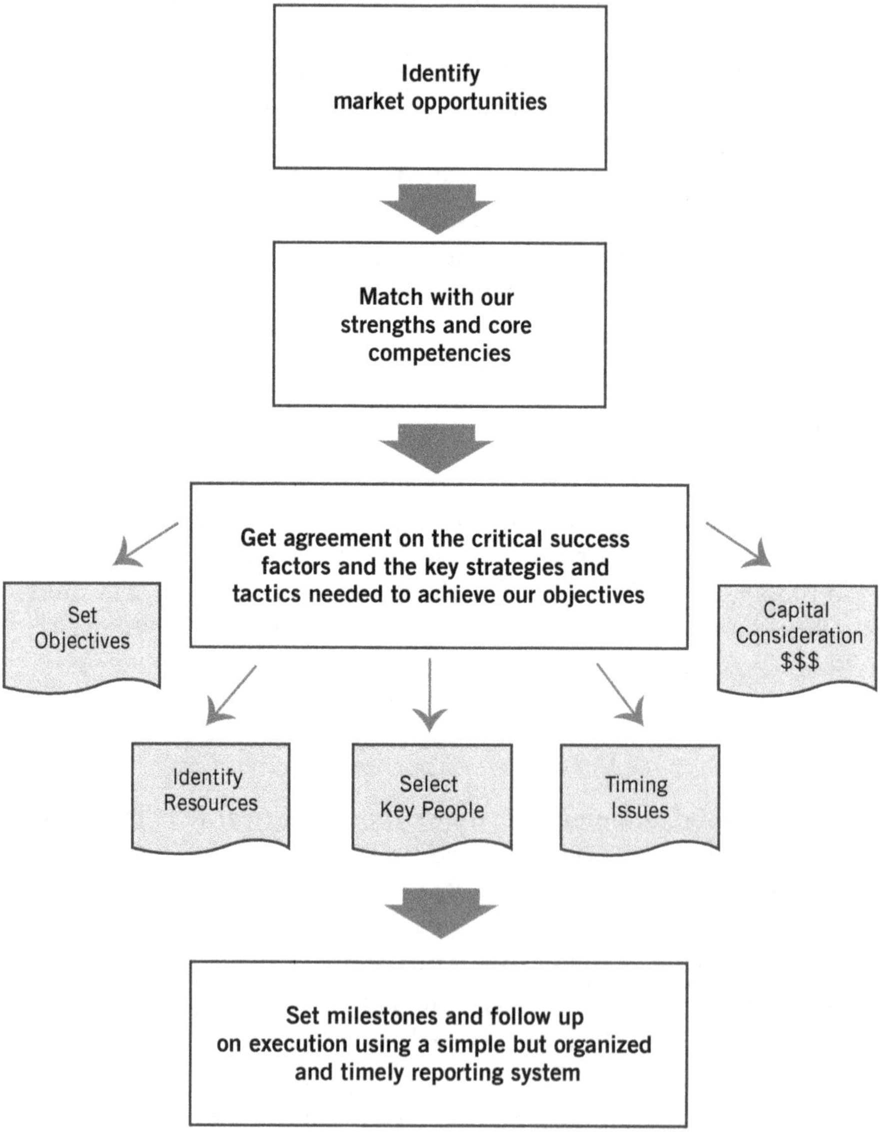

CHAPTER 4

BUSINESS PLANNING

"Always plan ahead. It wasn't raining when Noah built the ark."
— Richard Cushing

What is a business plan?

A business plan (BP) is a document that describes the future direction of a business. A business plan explains the business concept, summarizes the objectives/goals of the business, identifies the resources that will be used by the business and tells the reader why the business will succeed.

Business plans can be prepared for external or internal audiences. For external audiences, a business plan could be prepared for a bank to obtain financing or for investors to seek capital investment. Business plans prepared for internal audiences would focus on internal goals such as launching a new product or service, opening a new branch, buying new machinery and equipment and/or restructuring a department or division.

What's included in a business plan?

The content will vary according to the goals and the audience being targeted, but a business plan usually contains the following sections:

- **Executive summary:** Summarizes the key points of the business plan in one or two pages.
- **Overview:** Introduces the reader to the business.
- **Description of the products and services:** What does the company do? Tell the reader your line of business (e.g., retail, wholesale, manufacturing).
- **Overview of the industry:** Introduces the industry in which the business will compete.
- **Sales and marketing strategy:** Summarizes the product, promotion, pricing and distribution strategies of the business.
- **Description of management and staff:** Introduces the senior team (names, position, age, how long with the company, main responsibilities, and their professional experience).
- **Implementation plan:** Explains the milestones of the project or plan (how you will get from point A to point B to point C).
- **Financial plan:** Includes pro-forma balance sheets, income statements and cash flow statements. A balance sheet compares what your business owns to what it owes. A cash flow statement compares how much money is coming in to how much you spend. An income statement compares revenues to expenses to see if you are going to make money.

Business plans can vary in length from a few pages to over 100 pages. Although there are no hard and fast rules, I recommend that business plans should be between 15 pages and 25 pages in length.

To supplement the business plan, you can include such attachments as photos, articles, blueprints, illustrations, videos and brochures.

Internally focused business plans that target organizational goals may include a balanced scorecard or list of critical success factors. These things allow the success of the plan to be measured with non-financial indicators. These relatively new tools to monitor business performance also underline the confidence of the people who prepared the plan; they have already included suggested milestones to track the progress of the plan's execution.

Business plans that identify and target internal goals but provide only general guidance on how they will be met are called strategic plans. As we saw in the previous chapter, strategic plans usually cover the entire activity of an enterprise or organization, while business plans are generally more specific.

Here are more details about key sections to give you a feel for what type of information should be included in various sections of the business plan:

The executive summary

I think the executive summary is the most important section of the business plan. It can be described as the entry door of the plan.

A well-written executive summary must grab the attention of the reader, let them know what you do and what you want to achieve. It must give the reader a reason to read the whole document. It is a "pitch" that should convince the reader you have a great thing going, and it doesn't matter if they are granting approval, investing, agreeing or just providing their blessing.

I also suggest you write the executive summary last, even though this section is at the beginning of the plan. Ideally, the executive summary should be two or three pages.

You need to "knock out" your reader in the executive summary! Here is a suggested seven-punch approach:

1) Problem/opportunity
2) Our solution
3) Market assessment
4) Competition analysis
5) Fantastic team description
6) Financial information
7) Pinpoint milestones and the expected upward trend/reward

In the body of the business plan, you must support your problem/ opportunity with good research and provide evidence that your solution is both realistic and doable and that the market is attractive in size and direction. You have to show that you've done your homework on the competition, assembled a solid team and that the numbers are realistic, conservative and sound. Finally, you also must prove that the reward/ return on investment is lucrative.

The market assessment (point 3 above) in the executive summary should be in point form. Now, in the body of the business plan, you should go into more details and research to provide your assessment of the marketplace and the opportunities it provides. Here is a brief overview:

Market assessment

- Industry overview, estimated size of the market including trends and opportunities
- Legal/regulatory environment
- Target customer market segments
- Current and forecast sizes, and growth rates for relevant market segments
- Customer needs addressed by company's products, and by segment
- Profile of the customer-purchase process and purchase-decision criteria

Description of products, services and technologies

- Review of current/proposed products and technology
- R&D plan, milestones met and planned/product evolution plan
- Proprietary aspects/unique competitive advantages of product
- Protection of intellectual property
- Technology licensed
- Joint development agreements/technology alliances

Marketing

- Sales and marketing strategy
- Distribution channels, sales force
- Strategic alliance/distribution partners
- Promotion/pricing/support
- Key existing and/or prospective customers
- Projected market share

Competitive analysis

- Profile of products, strategy and resources of each major competitor
- Strengths and weaknesses of each major competitor
- Barriers to entry for new competitors

Operation/manufacturing

- Manufacturing/order-fulfillment strategy
- Facilities and equipment — current and planned
- Key suppliers and subcontractors, and alternative sources

Corporate organization/human resources

- Organization charts
- Number of staff by function
- Staffing plan and rationale for growth by department
- Compensation/remuneration plan
- Key employment agreements
- Job descriptions
- Corporate governance, board of directors, advisors

Finance

- Historical and five-year projected balance sheet, income statement and cash flows
- Monthly cash flows for 1–2 years
- Appropriate commentary, notes and assumptions
- Description of current capitalization (including options and warrants), investors/shareholders, creditors/bank lines

Investment opportunity

- Present and future funds sought, and proposed uses
- Preferred investment vehicle (e.g., common or preferred equity, convertible debt)
- Proposed valuation, rationale, and comparables (if available)

Summary of risks

- Key risks associated with each category above, with organization's contingency plan for mitigating each part

Appendices

- Management résumés, biographies, prior ventures
- References from customers, strategic partners
- Product literature
- Detailed financial schedules and assumptions
- Professional consultants: auditors, legal counsel, etc.
- Outstanding legal or regulatory disputes/issues

Why is a business plan important?

- The process of preparing a business plan will force you to think about your business, research some options, recognize opportunities and risks and test some of your assumptions.

- A business plan will help you identify the cash requirements of your business and the capital required (and the mix between equity and debt).
- A business plan can be used to raise funding from banks and investors.
- A business plan can be used to tell partners, management, employees, investors and others about your plans and strategies.
- A business plan provides a benchmark against which you compare the progress and performance of the business.

Typical structure for a business plan for a start-up venture

- Cover page and table of contents
- Executive summary
- Vision and mission statement
- Corporate values
- Business description
- Business environment analysis
- SWOT analysis (strengths-weaknesses-opportunities-threats)
- Industry background
- Competitor analysis
- Market analysis
- Sales and marketing plan
- Operations/production plan
- Management summary
- Financial plan
- List of advisors and references
- Attachments and milestones

In closing, remember, as Dr. Graeme Edwards said: "It is not the plan that is important, it's the planning."

CHAPTER 5

LEADERSHIP AND TEAM BUILDING

"Always do more than is required of you."
— George Patton

How do you define leadership?

Leadership has been described as "a process of social influence in which one person can enlist the aid and support of others in the accomplishment of a common task."[1] Other definitions describe a **leader** simply as "somebody whom people follow," or as "somebody who guides or directs others," while still others define leadership as "organizing a group of people to achieve a common goal."

I define leadership as the ability to lead people and to have people follow you. No matter what definition you like, studies about leadership have produced theories involving specific traits, behavior, power, vision and values, charisma, etc.

Over the years, many books have been written about leadership and leadership styles. They cover everything from an autocratic style to democratic style to a style that builds consensus.

---

1 Martin Chemers, *An Integrative Theory of Leadership* (Mahwah, NJ: Lawrence Erlbaum Associates, 1997), 1.

Looking for leadership traits

In the business and management arena, the key search is for the main leadership traits of a leader. What are the must-have skills for leaders? It is very important to know what traits we are looking for when we elect, choose or promote leaders.

Here is a short list of the most common traits:

1) The ability to **focus** on what is truly important: They must possess the skill of being able to identify the key strategic elements that are hidden in a sea of information.

2) The ability to **lead in a complex environment**: Leaders must be able to get things done. Do they have good ideas and can they get support from people for their ideas? Leaders must be able to marshal resources from people who work for them and from people who don't. They must be able to influence and convince others.

3) The ability to **communicate**: Leaders must be able to communicate with ease. In fact, this is a leader's most important tool. This involves telling people what is important and clearly communicating the need to get to the next level. Good communication is not necessarily putting together a good PowerPoint presentation or being a dazzling speaker or orator. It is the ability to effectively communicate your message to others.

4) The ability to **learn and to teach**: Leaders must be able to absorb information quickly and to dissipate information effectively. Leaders know their subject matter from every angle (i.e., strategically, tactically, technically, financially). Today's business environment and marketplace are evolving so rapidly that any blind spots are critical to the very survival of your business, never mind the success of your business.

5) The ability to be **authentic**: Some call it integrity or "value-based leadership." Being authentic means being straightforward. A leader must have values and stay true to them with their actions. This is commonly known as the ability to walk the talk!

Trust

While these five abilities are key traits of leadership, I believe the most important trait in leaders is **to be trusted**. I have seen strong, successful leaders who may not have all the above traits, but they led their organization to success because they were trustworthy and possessed integrity.

In my view, their strengths came from their ability to convey trust. A message that was almost subliminal was being communicated, and it conveyed that this man or woman can be trusted. Because of this, people will follow.

Many leaders can get respect or obtain followers from their position of authority. For example, a sergeant or officer in the army may get respect from the troops even if they have weak leadership skills. Leadership that is based on position or authority usually doesn't last.

Rapid turnover of the CEO position usually means poor selection of a leader. In some instances, a CEO may resign and before a successor has been named, the share price of the company's stock moves upward. WOW! The market is saying that this company is better off without its CEO! The opposite is true when a new CEO is appointed and the very same day the company's share price goes up. The new CEO hasn't even started to work, but the mere presence of the person has added shareholder value. Why? Their reputation alone is enough to positively influence the share price!

True leaders are those who continue to be leaders, regardless of their positions. This applies to strong leaders who continue to lead even when in jail or exile. Such examples may be extreme, but I want to underline the difference between true and genuine leadership and fake leadership. Genuine leadership is durable; fake leadership is temporary.

What does leadership look like?

Another important element to highlight in leadership is that strong leadership comes in different shapes and forms. Too often business leaders are described with a certain stereotypical look and feel, but true leadership comes in different profiles, forms and appearances.

Take Winston Churchill. He was a great leader who led Great Britain and the Allies to victory in the Second World War. He was short, fat and bald; he smelled of cigars and mumbled his words. Yet he was undeniably a strong leader who was able to lead his entire country through one of the most volatile times in history.

Every year, media organizations prepare a list of the strongest leaders in all areas of government, business, sports, philanthropy, etc. The choice of candidates always leads to arguments and disagreement.

The disagreement usually concerns leaders who may not be on the "good" side. Allow me to explain. Was Hitler a strong leader? How about Saddam Hussein? The answer is a definite yes! How you define good or bad may be personal, but you can have good and bad leaders leading both good and bad causes. Bad leaders might have good leadership skills, but if their cause is malignant, it will lead to something bad. Likewise, leaders with poor leadership skills won't be able to bring a good cause to fruition. With my definition, good leaders lead for a good cause and, in turn, they lead their people to a good and fruitful place.

Developing leaders

Is leadership an art, a science or a combination of the two? Are we born with the gift of leadership or do we acquire this ability through experience and study? While opinions may vary, I believe the answer is a combination of both.

Some people are naturally gifted to lead with ease while others have to work harder at being a leader. Being an introvert or extrovert is not the key criterion, but people born with a leadership gene in their DNA can improve their leadership skills with practice and experience. However, the lack of leadership DNA is difficult to acquire through study.

Without a doubt, history has taught us that leaders tend to grow their leadership skills as they acquire experience through success and failure, and by going through challenges that test their stamina and maturity.

I believe that you must have some initial leadership DNA, and then you can perfect it and develop it through practice. It would be difficult to become a leader only through learning without having some in-born traits.

Who is at the helm makes all the difference

Top leaders, whether they are presidents of nations, corporations, institutions or sports teams, set the tone of their organizations and greatly influence the results of their teams.

A strong leader of a country enters history forcefully and leaves a legacy behind, while a weak leader merits only a cursory mention or isn't mentioned at all. A strong sports coach leads the team to success and becomes a sports legend while weak coaches are quickly forgotten. Similarly, in business, a strong CEO helps the corporation build a strong name brand and increase shareholder value over time, while a weak CEO can weaken the brand and deplete shareholder value.

In business how can you evaluate good leadership and good management?

Strong leaders and CEOs are easily recognizable by their corporate results. Here is my short list for recognizing strong performance:

1) Consistently **strong financial results** year in and year out do not happen because of luck. They happen as a result of good planning and excellent execution.
2) A proven record of **allocating capital** to successful projects that bring healthy profits and help grow shareholder value.
3) A consistent **strengthening of the moat** around the business that does not allow competitors to score important points.
4) The creation of **solid, long-term, win-win partnerships** not only with customers, but with employees, shareholders and vendors. In other words, creating a strong partnership with all stakeholders.
5) Lastly but most importantly, creating and growing a **brand that is trusted** and liked.

Ask the right questions

In business, strong leaders should have strong boards. Here is a list of seven simple questions that can help you evaluate the stewardship level of a board:

1) Are investments and acquisitions in line with the company's core competitive strengths, or do they exist merely to diversify the business? Diversifications may help reduce the overall business risk, but they also create complexity at the top of the organization and are difficult to manage over the long term.
2) Does the corporation have a history of taking impairment charges, and frequent reorganizations and restructurings? This is usually an indication of weak strategy, and the need to constantly fix and cover past mistakes.
3) Is the corporation aiming to create long-term shareholder value or is it only concerned about quarterly earnings?
4) Is the corporation building its brand and reputation or is it just focused on profitability? Is the corporation widening its moat or losing ground to the competition?
5) Does the corporation pay a dividend? While opinions will vary on this point, I personally prefer corporations that pay a yearly dividend to shareholders. The size of the dividend is not as important as the principle of paying a dividend that increases in line with the growth of the business. On a personal note, I have noticed that over time corporations that usually pay a dividend have stronger boards.
6) How is the level of compensation of the corporation? How does the compensation of the top ten executives of the company compare with the average pay? Excessive executive compensation is a sign of a weak board, poor stewardship and potential HR problems for the future.
7) Are the CEO and senior executive team open and forthcoming about present challenges and future opportunities? Or are missteps and bad news swept under the carpet? I like to read an annual report written by business people and not by PR specialists who talk and say nothing!

Team building is an art

It may surprise you, but team building is an art more so than a set formula. Strong leaders know how to attract, develop, motivate and retain powerful teams. This is especially difficult when your team is made of strong leaders. Think of my earlier analogy with a good soccer team. You need not only good players in every position, but people who can work together so the team wins. In this way you don't merely have individual players showing off their abilities. That isn't a team.

With a soccer team you need a good goalkeeper, good defence, good midfield and good attack. In addition, you need a second good goalkeeper who doesn't mind staying on the bench for most games. You also need to have good players in reserve who are ready when the main players can't play because of injuries or other reasons. As well, you need players who submit to authority and who put team objectives ahead of their own individual goals. In a business team, it's not much different. Inability to develop these strong team traits will result in bickering among team members and conflict and communication silos.

A strong leader can weave a solid team together and continue to manage it with recruitment, promotion and substitution. Sometimes, you have to let go of key players in order to preserve the strengths of the team and to continue building a stronger team in the future.

Poor team players have no room on a strong team. The strength of a successful team is derived from strong, individual players, not from one or two strong players.

A good example was the FIFA World Cup of 2014 when Germany won. While Germany did not have the best star players, it did have the best team. Other teams relied on one or two star players to make the difference, but in the end, the strongest team won.

For tennis or golf, it is individual ability that matters, but for soccer, football, hockey, baseball and basketball, it is team play that makes the difference between winning and losing. It is the difference between a gold or bronze medal and not getting on the podium at all. Business performance is the same; it is team performance that separates winners from losers, and the excellent from the mediocre.

You can't rely on past achievements. You may learn from past successes and failures, but you must keep your eye on the future, and on what that future needs for you to succeed.

CHAPTER 6

RECRUITING THE RIGHT TALENT

Human Resources

"The greatest vision and the best strategy
are neither here nor there without a great team."
— Hugh Latif

Human resources fundamentals for selection and recruiting

At the core of every successful company is a team of talented and qualified people.

This team includes an executive contingent with the experience and expertise to grow and direct the company forward. It also includes a management group with the knowledge and hiring ability to skillfully select the right people, and then place them in the right position in every level of the organization.

Organizations rarely run themselves, no matter how top-heavy they are; they still need key players (without big titles) who perform at a high level in every area. In this chapter we will cover the key ingredients for making successful hires and what homework you need to do to attract qualified human resources to your organization.

The essential points are outlined below. This is a powerful list of ten fundamental principles. Applying them to your human resources recruitment missions should improve your ability to hire the right candidates.

1) Do you have a job description?

A job description can be a one-page document or an elaborate document with a lot of details that includes job responsibilities, tasks, type of decisions to be made, safety issues or health requirements. But don't be intimidated by this. If you do not have a job description for the position, start with a simple one-page document and build content as you progress.

Your first document does not need to be elaborate. A single page including job title, who the position reports to, a simple overview of the position and main responsibilities should be enough.

For senior positions, the job description can be relatively general, but for junior positions it must have specific information about duties and tasks. However, whether for a senior or junior position, the job-description document must give a clear understanding of what the job entails in straightforward language.

You can search the Internet for sample job descriptions for almost any position and get several samples online. If writing is not your strength, consultants who specialize in job-description writing and editing are available at reasonable rates. HR consultants can also be effectively used to help you develop an inventory of the needed job descriptions for your organization. The key is that job descriptions spell out what each job entails and how that position fits in the overall organization. This is an important document that should not be overlooked.

2) Do you have an applicant profile?

This is a one-page document that includes the key qualifications you are looking for, such as years of experience, specific skills, level of education-and job requirements. The document may also contain the salary range and a brief description of the benefits and incentives, if applicable.

Often, matching applicant skills with the job requirements requires some tradeoffs. In descending order of priority, decide the qualifications and character attributes that the ideal candidate should possess, and then specify what criteria are absolutely essential from your list of priorities.

Personal characteristics are also key to getting the person with the right attributes for a position. It is imperative that the personal attributes of a person be in line with the job requirements. For example, an introverted individual may have great analytical skills, but would not enjoy a job that includes customer service and handing complaints, while an extrovert may not have analytical skills but they could be a people person who enjoys serving customers and resolving complaints. Some people enjoy working on the telephone while others dislike it. Some enjoy travel while others don't. An applicant profile should describe not only the qualifications, but also personal attributes.

3) Who are you hiring? Is it for a managerial or non-managerial position?

Be careful if you are hiring for a **managerial position** (e.g., supervisor, executive, director). Fight the urge to rush into filling an important position even if the need seems urgent. Invest the time and good methods it takes to find the right person for the position.

You can always appoint an "acting manager" as an interim solution until your search finds the best candidate to lead your department or team. Putting the right person in a managerial position is important because they provide leadership to others and can influence or deflate productivity and team morale on a broad scale.

If you are hiring for a **non-managerial** position, it's still important to employ good methodology and take time, but you don't have to look for supervisory or managerial skills. A worker who has difficulty meeting the quota can be trained or given more time to improve their productivity, but hiring a manager with no managerial skills will damage the department or team they are supposed to lead. Mistakes can easily be corrected for a non-management worker, but a bad managerial hire will take more time to fix.

The latter statement may seem counter-intuitive, however, the reality is that for non-managerial positions the pressure and demands of day-to-day operations may require a quick hiring solution. Also take into account that this individual's influence will be contained to that specific position. Please do not think I am cutting corners. I am just being practical. Here is an example to illustrate my point. If you have one weak player in a soccer team of 11 players, you still have 10 strong players. But if you have a weak coach or a weak captain, the performance of the entire team will almost certainly suffer.

4) What is the first priority?

The first priority is integrity and ethics. Never hire a candidate whom you think has questionable integrity and/or ethics. No matter how qualified and experienced the candidate appears to be, integrity and ethics are a must. This rule applies to the most junior position in the company just as much as it does to the president or general manager. Do not cut corners in this critical area. You can train a person for the duties and tasks of the position, but you will have a very hard time indeed changing that person's integrity and ethics.

5) Leadership ability or technical skills?

If you are hiring for a managerial position, leadership ability and people skills should be your second priority behind integrity and ethics. Technical knowledge is also important, but secondary to leadership skills. The main requirement for hiring a manager is an individual with a strong ability to manage people and resources in order to achieve set objectives.

People and communication skills are key requirements in any management position. I have never seen a good manager who was not a good communicator, just as I have never seen a good manager who was not a people person. Managers must be good communicators and possess excellent people skills. The technical part can be learned with time, but integrity, ethics and leadership are all difficult to learn.

6) Consider the "Stretch Factor"

The "Stretch Factor" is the degree of stretching that the applicant needs to go through in order to get the job done. Perhaps the applicant is overqualified and can perform well without much effort. In this case, the very low stretch level may cause the applicant to be very comfortable in the new position, which may quickly lead to loss of interest and end in rapid turnover.

A very high stretch factor may cause you to destroy the applicant if their skills are stretched too far to do the job. Try to strike a good balance between hiring a candidate who is challenged by the position, but not overwhelmed by the responsibilities.

Here are some examples:

The manager of a team of 50 people may stretch to manage 100 or even 500 people (i.e., operations 2x to 10x larger). But they may have difficulties adjusting to 10,000 people, which is a stretch of 100 or 200x).

Similarly, a manager responsible for a $10M business unit may find it feasible to manage a $50M or $100M business unit (5x or 10x larger). However, a $500M or more business unit (50x larger) may be too much of a stretch.

There is no rule of thumb for the right formula, but you should keep the stretch factor in mind when estimating the applicant's ability to perform.

7) The five key areas to cover in selection and recruiting

a) **Applicant details:** This includes the facts about what the applicant has done earlier. For example, what were the positions held in previous jobs? Who did the applicant report to? What were the dates, responsibilities and span of management? Look for stability, professional growth and promotions — things that indicate the applicant's level of drive and professionalism.

b) **Applicant qualifications:** Consider the assignments held, achievements, missions, challenges and setbacks. Did applicants have similar missions in their past work? How did they do with opportunities and challenges? Let them give you examples. Let them describe a typical day and a typical week. What do I mean by missions? For example, if an applicant had turnaround missions/assignments in the past, they should know something about turnarounds. If that is their mission in your organization, it would be a definite plus.

If an applicant has such experience in turnarounds, but your organization is not in need of one, then this experience is helpful but not necessary. Your organization may be looking for someone who will drive growth, so it would be good to find someone who has achieved growth in past positions. If your organization has achieved tremendous growth and now needs to "digest" this rapid growth, then you need to search for an organizer and builder who can consolidate the acquired growth. Watch for stability or instability — rapid turnover of jobs — and ask questions.

A history of stable employment and the contrary (a history of "hopping around") both demonstrate personal attributes you should take note of. Ask for the "why" behind both stability and instability.

c) **Applicant character:** This covers personality traits that match with their position requirements. Is the applicant an introvert, an extrovert, an analytical person or a people person? Do they possess leadership skills? How do they make decisions? Are they organized? How do they handle authority? Can they accept working under authority? What about creativity or problem-solving? Can they work with deadlines? Can they handle several assignments simultaneously? Do they have project management skills? Are they a good team player?

   Evaluating character and personality is a key component of good recruitment. Generally, people will do what they have done in the past, so hire people with the strengths required for the job. Don't hire people on the assumption that they will change. You can train people in certain tasks, technicalities or processes, but you can seldom change people's character. In other words, don't hire a guitar player to play piano. Hire a guitar player for a more important guitar role or to join a more successful band.

d) **Applicant fit:** See if the applicant is a good fit with the existing team and with the company's subculture. It's also worth considering how well the working relationship with their immediate boss might be. This is a very sensitive area, but key to a successful hire.

   What is the "chemistry" between two people? It is that indescribable thing that makes two people flow together or clash for no particular reason. Never hire someone without having them interviewed by their immediate superior. Wrong chemistry can destroy good teams and result in poor performance. It can also sabotage an excellent hire, so watch for good chemistry between the applicant and their direct superior, and between the applicant and the team.

e) **Others:** Other factors to consider are reference checks, remuneration, career path and what I call a three-to-five-year plan. A thorough reference check is a must in order to find out previous performance and conduct. Ideally, reference checking should not be done by a clerk, but a knowledgeable HR person. Or the reference check may be carried out by the manager or the candidate's superior. Why? A clerk might miss important vocal cues or "body language" shown by the reference giver. Body language over the telephone you ask? Most definitely! A few seconds of hesitation before answering a question, avoiding answering a question or reluctance to give examples are clues that can be very revealing during a reference check, even over the telephone.

Remuneration for a new position should always be higher, so recruiters need to find out if the remuneration package is motivating or a downward or lateral move. Does the position offered represent a forward step in the applicant's career or is it a regressive move? Can the applicant continue to learn and grow for at least three years in the new position? What are the medium- and long-term career goals of the applicant, and can they fulfill them for your organization? Always remember that you are looking for talented individuals to join your group. Your organization will be strengthened by people who are growing and who have a passion for what your organization does. Seniority and long-term service should be strengths for your organization.

8) Initial screening of candidates

An initial screening of candidates can be done through a review of the résumé and a quick preliminary telephone interview. Spend time with the résumés you have received and try to read between the lines. Make sure you check for gaps of employment, the presentation of the résumé and overall feel of the résumé.

This initial screening should allow you to organize the candidates into three categories. Category A contains the must-see applicants (i.e., applicants who look qualified on paper and who meet your requirements). Category B consists of the back-up applicants for those in Category A.

Category C is reserved for applicants whose qualifications are simply not adequate to meet the requirements of the position. The telephone interview helps you refine your preliminary selection and should not last more than 10–15 minutes.

The telephone interview is a quick screening of some basic areas such as: applicant telephone manners, basic communication skills, initial first impression and key criteria not usually in a typical résumé. Examples may include a driver's license, physical condition, ability to travel or willingness to work weekends.

The telephone interview role is to prepare for a productive face-to-face interview. It complements the entire recruitment and selection process, but is no substitute for the face-to-face interview.

9) The personal interview

- Prepare for the interview by making notes, jotting down the questions you want to ask and important points of discussion.
- Prepare a favorable setting for the interview. You can do this by limiting interruptions (i.e., turn off phones, inform front-desk staff that you will be busy for the time allotted for the interview, tacking a note onto the office door). Put the applicant at ease and do your best to provide an atmosphere in which your candidate can relax and put their best foot forward.
- Do not talk too much during the interview. A good ratio to keep in mind is the 80/20 rule, where the candidate is talking 80% of the time and the interviewer asks questions 20% of the time. Take a few minutes to put the candidate at ease. Give a quick overview of the job and the company, and also the agenda for the interview itself. Ask key questions and get the candidates to respond and to talk about themselves.
- Ask all the candidates the same questions so you can compare their answers. Use your checklist and make notes as you go along.
- Make sure your questions are strategic and designed to find out whether the person is qualified for the position. One simple strategy is to ensure that questions are open-ended and to avoid yes/no answers. Questions should be constructed to give you deeper insight into a candidate's thinking and their probable behavior, and a good idea of how they think on their feet and handle problem solving.
- Keep the focus of the interview in view. Stay away from off-topic discussions that do not enhance your understanding of the candidate. Try to prevent the interview from turning into an interrogation or a chat session by keeping control, but without stemming its natural flow.
- Do not forget that there are many recruitment laws that prohibit discrimination in employment on the grounds of a number of criteria including race, color, ethnic origin, sex, age and marital status. The list

is extensive and continues to be amended, so contact the labor department of your federal government to get the latest HR manual, which will include off-limit questions for interviews. Employment decisions should be based on the applicant's ability to do the job, not on factors unrelated to the job.

- One of my favorite ways to interview is to ask the candidate the following question: "Take me through your career briefly after you graduated from university in [x year]." This allows the applicant to describe what they feel is important and to volunteer a lot of information. I then interrupt tactfully and diplomatically to ask about specific things. Examples would include: Who did you report to in that job? If I called them, what would they say about your performance in that job? How would they describe you? How big is the company? Annual sales? Total employees? What did you like about that job? What did you learn most at this company? This method of interviewing gives the applicant the feeling of freedom in explaining their qualifications and expertise. At the same time, I can gather specific information for clarification through my questions.

10) Make up your mind

It's decision-making time! Do not take too long to make up your mind. You can lose good candidates if you procrastinate. After you have taken the time to do your homework, make a decision promptly.

In addition to these ten rules and suggestions, I can also share other ideas about selection and recruitment:

1) **Brief interview with team members:** It is good practice to have the applicant meet some of the team members they will work with for a few minutes. This gives the applicant an opportunity to get a feel for the team and the company culture. This brief introduction to their potential team and company will not be comprehensive, but it gives the applicant a taste of what to expect. Likewise, team members who have an opportunity to spend time with the applicant feel involved in the selection process, and this may be important for team-building down the road.

2) **The 80/20 rule:** The talent marketplace can be described as consisting of 80% of people not looking for a job and 20% of people who are looking for a job. When you place a recruitment advertisement, you are searching within the 20% category. If you have a way to access that 80% pool of people who are not looking for a job, that's even more effective.

   Executive search firms and headhunters are supposed to take their search into this 80% category, but they often don't. How can you effectively extend your search into this 80% category? You can search this 80% category by subscribing to sites such as LinkedIn, or through access to specialized private databases of associations, networking organizations, directories, etc. While this may involve more work, it can be very effective in locating exceptional candidates. Obviously, this method of recruitment would be more justified for senior positions in your organization or for specific positions with hard-to-find specifications and experience.

3) **HR tests:** Another hiring tool is HR evaluation methods or psychological tests. Do they work? Are they effective? There is a wide array of these methods and tests available, and while I do not know all of them, I have used several in my career. However, in general I have not been overly impressed with them. My experience with psychometric tools is that they are good in confirming my conclusions, but have rarely yielded an unforeseen revelation with direct bearing on my decision-making process. One exception is the *Birkman Method©*, which took me by surprise since it identifies with incredible ease not only a person's strengths and weaknesses, but their areas of stress, how they make decisions, how they are likely to behave, how they relate to others, how they deal with change or acceptance of authority or team interaction. *The Birkman Method©* can give you incredible insights into people. It is a great tool when you are **recruiting** or **promoting** people. Most importantly, the information provided by the *Birkman Method©* shows how to best **manage** each person on your team and how to place each team member in the **right position**.

Making the correct people decisions (selection, promotion, team play, etc.) is key to a successful managerial and executive career. In my opinion, the ability to select the right people, develop them, motivate them and make them work in winning teams is the most important requirement for success. HR evaluation methods could be used to complement your own evaluation, but should not substitute for your experience in selection and recruitment work.

CHAPTER 7

EFFECTIVE COMMUNICATION FOR SUCCESSFUL EXECUTIVES

"The single biggest problem in communication is the illusion that it has taken place."
— George Bernard Shaw

Effective communication is the backbone of successful leadership. It is the most powerful ingredient for managing those you lead. It doesn't matter if you are a general manager, a GM in training, an entrepreneur or a CEO, your success as a leader will be influenced by your ability to communicate effectively.

Almost any position requires some kind of leadership, and leadership depends on effective communication. Effective communication is important when you want to make convincing presentations with confidence, negotiate with ease or resolve conflicts quickly.

The ability to get your message across effectively and clearly is vital. But it's more than that. Communication is involved in how you set goals and objectives, communicate with staff and train and develop people. It's part of instructing, encouraging, correcting, presenting, coaching and rewarding others.

Are we born with the gift of good communication or do we acquire it through experience and study? That is a good question. My experience indicates that some are born with this ability while others have to work hard at it. What I mean is that for some of us communication flows naturally but for others it must be more intentional.

Here is an important point to remember. What I am about to share with you can benefit both types of people. Paying attention to the key components of communication will make you a better communicator whether you are a natural-born communicator or one who has to learn to hone that skill.

Let's simplify this by rating communication skills on a scale of one to ten. I hope that following and implementing these practical suggestions will move your score up by two to four points or more on the communication scale. No matter where your starting point is, you can improve your score by reflecting on these suggestions and putting them into action.

PERSONAL COMMUNICATION

Communicating Clearly

Motivating people, gaining the trust of your team or customers, managing change and negotiating successfully all require clear communication. Clear communication means that people understand what you say and what your expectations are of them. If people tell you, "I am sorry I misunderstood" or "Oh . . . is that what you meant?" then you may want to review your communication style.

Here are three easy steps to achieve clearer communication:

1) **Prepare ahead of time.** Think beforehand what you want to communicate, whether it is at a meeting, on the telephone or through an email or whatever medium you are using. Think first and then organize your message.
2) Take the time to **clearly explain the message** you are communicating. Do you need examples, photos or documents to reinforce your message? Ask the person or group for confirmation of what they understood from your message. Be diplomatic, but a timely, quick confirmation is a sign of caring, and it also emphasizes that communication is a two-way process.
3) **Follow up** in due time to make sure the message has been received correctly.

Achieving clarity starts by being clear in your own mind about what you want to communicate and to whom. Try to eliminate ambiguity or potential misunderstandings when relaying information, ideas or instructions by being brief, concise and to the point.

As we discussed in an earlier chapter, executives and senior managers have three key responsibilities when leading teams:

1) Delivering **results**.
2) Strengthening the **strategic position** of their company, division, department or team.
3) **Developing** their people skills and **building** a strong team.

Effective communication is the most important ingredient in achieving these three key responsibilities.

If you are not effective at delegating, it is only a matter of time before you hit a brick wall because you can't do everything yourself. Many team leaders are workaholics and many end up stressed and burnt out due to lack of proper delegation. It doesn't matter how strategically minded you are or how smart you are. You need to get those you lead to execute your strategy with excellence, and to do this you need to communicate this strategy with effectiveness.

Part of communicating clearly also means using the appropriate vehicle. There are many different tools at your disposal for enhancing your communication. They include face-to-face communication, meetings, telephone, email, writing, speaking, town hall meetings, formal and informal events, breakfasts, lunches and dinners.

Learning to be a good listener

Is it easier to talk or listen? Because we have two ears and one mouth, it should be easier to listen, but I bet you agree that it takes effort and training to be a good listener!

Learning to listen is also part of being an effective communicator. Listening is not the same as hearing. Hearing is the sound you hear, while listening requires focus and paying attention not only to what is being said but to *how* it is being said. A good listener will also listen to what is not said.

Becoming a good listener requires some basic principles. Here are five key points:

1) Stop talking! While this may be obvious, it is important. A general rule of thumb in situations where listening is important is to use the 80/20 rule. This means that you listen 80% of the time and you speak or ask questions 20% of the time.
2) Be prepared to listen. Take interest in what is said to you. Take interest in the person who is talking to you.
3) Maintain eye contact whenever possible.
4) Remove any distractions or potential distractions that may disrupt your listening. In addition to mobile phones, telephones or the presence of other people, this could include someone who speaks with a heavy accent, the tempo people are talking with, loud volume or lack of privacy.
5) Pay attention to non-verbal cues such as facial expressions, body language/gestures, tone, eye contact and key words.

INTERNAL COMMUNICATION (For organizations/companies)

As an entrepreneur, executive or manager, it is essential for you to use key events to update those you lead on things like company achievements, performance appraisals and future goals. A summer BBQ or Christmas party are excellent occasions to do this and they provide opportunities to thank and encourage the staff.

Send a **one-page letter to all employees** every quarter. This helps them stay up-to-date on the company's performance and informs them about future goals. Posting the letter on the bulletin board is all right, but it is more effective to attach the letter to the pay statement or check. This ensures that every employee receives the letter and knows about it.

Meeting new employees for a quick breakfast within their first 30–60 days of employment is exceptionally informative both for you and them. You will learn about your recruiting and selection procedures, company training systems, frontline managers' behavior, productivity and quality measures, and get suggestions free of charge. Most importantly, you will learn first-hand about the calibre of people who are joining your team.

Performance reviews, employee awards, employee suggestion programs and **sales lead programs** are all excellent tools in the quest to promote internal communication. Don't depend on your human resources manager to manage these HR tools. Take the time to review these tools periodically with your managers. Find out if suggestions are increasing or decreasing.

Select a few suggestions and ask to see what answers were provided, who provided them and how long it took management to respond. Find out if sales leads are being used by the sales force and how successful they are. Ask the sales-lead providers if they were thanked for submitting the sales leads, and if they received their commission.

These tools will motivate your staff, boost team morale, enhance effective teamwork and spur staff to be dedicated to customer satisfaction. These tools help make the sales department, operations or production departments work effectively together.

Performance reviews that are well executed and well managed help managers and staff work together better and avoid the "us vs. them" mentality. That sort of thing often creates invisible walls, which in turn inhibit creativity and performance.

Frequent celebrations for exceptional performance, significant achievements by the staff and achieving key milestones help build staff confidence and help keep things in perspective in a competitive marketplace that is filled with increasing customer expectation. Take the opportunity of a special event and make it a mini celebration by offering a pizza lunch to the department or staff. Celebrate a major win like a new record for productivity in the plant or the acquisition of a strategic new customer by making a small speech. This is when you compliment the teamwork, open a bottle of champagne and distribute free gift cards. Whatever is acceptable in the company culture is a great communication tool.

A **suggestion program** also helps employees think about how to improve the business. The people on the frontline with customers or who carry out the actual work (those on the assembly line, in the warehouse, in the delivery truck or behind the computer) are always your best source of suggestions. You must encourage your employees to be proactive in thinking about improvements, and encourage them to find solutions that work both for them and the company as a whole.

You must also reward them for their input, and the reward does not always have to be monetary. There are many ways to reward people. It doesn't matter if you manage a large company with several hundred employees or a small family business with a handful of them.

What most motivates people is recognition.

You can reward your employees and recognize their achievements in many ways. Public and private praise can be in the form of thank-you cards, gift cards, buying lunch, a merchandise gift or gift card or a subscription to their favorite magazine. Most of all, make sure you tell people how good you feel about what they did, and how it helps the organization and the team. Encourage them to do more of the same good work. Be specific and genuine.

Finally, with regards to internal communication, it is vital that you **meet once a month with your senior team** to review the results vs. the plan. Do this to evaluate what decisions need to be made and what action must be taken in order to accelerate or sustain your performance. This helps gauge if you are on track or need to turn things around if you are behind. Separate meetings with team members can address specific issues, but there is no substitute for a monthly meeting where senior team members learn how the team is doing corporately.

Keep in mind that developing your people and building a strong team are key responsibilities of a good leader. Use these team meetings to develop the leadership skills of team members. These skills include public speaking, being accountable, taking responsibility, decision making, planning, communicating, problem solving, meeting deadlines, setting objectives, handling human resources issues and resolving conflicts.

Downward, upward and lateral communication

Before I leave the subject of personal and internal communication, I want to explain the different types of internal communication (i.e., downward communication, upward communication, lateral communication).

Downward communication is communication from a manager to members of the team. Upward communication is communication from you to your immediate superior/boss. Lateral communication is communication from you to your colleagues in the company. The content and approach will differ depending on the direction of the communication, and this must be taken into account when crafting your communication strategy.

Equally important is knowing the difference between communication that seeks to simply **inform**, communication that seeks to **obtain approval** and communication that gives a **direct order or instruction**.

Look at the difference between these examples:

- I am writing to **inform** you that we have opened a new office in . . .
- I am pleased to **announce** the appointment of Mary King to the position of . . .
- I am writing to seek your **approval** over the purchase of . . .
- I am looking forward to your **support** for the project . . .
- I am writing to remind you that I am waiting for your **written authorization** for . . ..
- I am writing to **inform** you that effective May 5, xxxx . . .
- I am writing to **invite** you to our meeting of . . . on the subject of . . . Please come prepared with . . .
- I am writing to seek your specific **feedback** on . . . Thank you for responding by email by Thursday . . . so that I can . . .

EXTERNAL COMMUNICATION

External communication involves effective communication to and with the marketplace, customers, prospects, suppliers, bankers, media, governments and competitors. Your company's goodwill is not only based on sales and profits, but also includes your company's reputation within the marketplace. It is important to know what customers and suppliers think of you, and what message you are actually conveying to the world.

Everything used externally communicates something to the marketplace. This includes your business cards, brochures, letters, website, signs, invoices, envelopes, product packaging and even your check and packing slip.

Every piece of paper coming from you directly or indirectly sends a message.

The organization's reception area, office, plant, warehouse, signage and parking lot all communicate a message. Is your reception area clean and attractive? Is the telephone answered quickly and professionally? In this sense, external communication can be powerful and it often happens in an entirely passive state. Remember that you never get a second chance to make that first impression. This is why frontline and front-desk staff, and their environment, are key participants in your organization's external communication.

You can use those moments that visitors spend in your reception area to communicate subliminally. For example, display awards the company has won. Exhibit photos of your product(s) or key staff members. Show any community initiatives you contributed to, along with certificates of membership in associations. All these things help communicate that your business is well established, proud of its contribution, helpful in the local community and successful.

A clean visitors washroom will also be remembered by people who may have traveled far to get to your office. A small bouquet of fresh flowers (have them picked up or delivered) or a bowl of candy on the receptionist's desk add a nice finishing touch in making waiting time in your reception area pleasant. Making your work environment clean, safe and attractive sends a clear message to employees, customers and visitors alike.

In most companies, communication with the external world happens largely through telephone and email. Again, it is an excellent investment to provide specific training to your employees about professional telephone manners. This includes the use of voicemail and recorded messages, how to transfer calls and how to leave effective voicemails. In this manner, not only do you train your people to be more effective and productive, but you impress customers and business associates with the high calibre of professionals you employ in the company.

I always get positive comments and praise regarding how professional and friendly my assistants who answer the office telephone are. I am told how they go beyond the call of duty to help callers with their needs, or inform them of my whereabouts if I am away, or take important messages or suggest my voicemail.

Don't underestimate the importance of a good receptionist and a welcome and friendly voice when people are trying to reach you. Here is another important note. Always try to take your calls, even when you know it is a sales call! I know some of you will not agree, but here is why I think it is important. First, you may be interested in what the caller has to offer. Second, you may turn around the situation and identify an opportunity.

Finally, I believe that even if you have no interest in the caller's product or service, you should be the one who says "thanks but no thanks." It should not be your assistant. In other words, don't hire gatekeepers. Be open to the world, and once you know the specific message, be selective.

The same suggestion applies to proper use of the email system, which can be a great productivity booster (or productivity bandit) for your organization. Companies invest vast amounts of money to purchase and install the latest technological devices and software but then fail to invest in training people how to best use this technology.

Investing in training is a profitable proposition because it helps your staff be efficient in their role as they use the technology in order to make things faster, more efficient and organized. More on this can be found in the training chapter. But here are some simple do's and don'ts about email protocol:

Email ABCs

1) Don't answer your email throughout the day. It is distracting and contagious, steals your ability to concentrate and makes you unable to differentiate between the important, the urgent and the priority. Dedicate specific times during the day to read your emails and respond to them.
2) When answering an email, think first, think again and then choose the appropriate words. Never allow your emotions to run wild. Manage your emotions and select appropriate vocabulary.
3) Remember that email is an official communication tool.
4) Respond, don't react is excellent advice.
5) Use blind-copy email in specific situations but not as a general rule.
6) Copy only those who need to receive the information. If you want to send it for FYI (for your information) purposes, forward your message and put in the subject "FYI."

7) When replying to an email, change the subject as needed. Don't merely reply using the sender subject unless the subject is the same. If the subject has indeed changed, change the subject to best reflect the content of your email.
8) Email is public domain, so never use profanity or bad language. A good rule of thumb is that if what you are saying needs to remain confidential or reserved, then email is not the right tool for the message.
9) Always acknowledge receipt of your emails even with a simple thank-you note in the subject, which takes seconds.
10) Have a signature on your outgoing email with your name, position, company, contact details and company logo. This makes it easy for the recipient to know immediately who has sent them the email and how to contact you. Some people attach a disclaimer and that's OK if it is brief.

Your marketing engine

Make sure your marketing machine also communicates the right message to the marketplace. This means a professional and attractive website, an attractive trade-show stand, corporate events that are professionally executed and press releases that are well written. A professional, attractive and friendly website is an effective tool that communicates to the marketplace why people should do business with you. For more on this consult the online presence chapter.

Websites are open for business 24/7. The size of the computer screen and/or the mobile phone or tablet will always level the playing field between you and larger companies, especially from a communication standpoint. The IBM website is viewed on the same monitor as your website. It depends on you to captivate potential customers and/or visitors by making your website user-friendly, interactive and informative. A website that is well executed and well maintained can be one of the best tools to support your sales and marketing engine. It should also have links to relevant social-media sites. This will help give you that slight edge and differentiate you from competitors.

A final word. Your membership and affiliation with reputable organizations and trade associations will help you and your team build their professional networks, and get your message and brand out to those who can influence your business. A consistent and professional message is your key to success.

There is no doubt that effective communication skills are key to your success as a general manager, an entrepreneur or a CEO. While the organization size can add more challenges in keeping communication flowing properly, the suggestions in this chapter are effective and applicable to large and small organizations alike.

CHAPTER 8

MANAGING PEOPLE

How to Get Above-Average Results from Average People

"People never care how much you know
until they know how much you care."
— John C. Maxwell

Many times during my career I would hear executives say, "We need a different kind of people." This implied that their people did not have the right qualifications. These same executives would conclude that to change the situation they must start to recruit better people.

I agree that growth often brings a new need for more experience and more specific expertise. But the skill of recruiting the right talent, developing people, creating teamwork and managing people with excellence are the real keys for success. There are no good people and bad people. People perform well when they do what they like and turn in a poor performance if they are in the wrong job. The key is not to have extraordinary people; the key is to get extraordinary results from average people.

I once spoke with a high-rise window cleaner and asked him what he enjoyed about his job. He told me this was his best job ever and went on to explain that it was quiet and serene up there. He didn't have a boss breathing over his shoulder and no people to distract him. He worked in the fresh air and could listen to his favorite music and, best of all, the pay was very good. Wow! It struck me that nothing about this job would attract a person like me. To be hanging from a cable like salami with no people contact all day is certainly not my kind of job no matter how well it pays.

Another time I interviewed a young lady who worked in a funeral parlor. Her job as an embalmer was to prepare bodies for their last viewing. She enjoyed dressing them up and doing their makeup for the last time. What a job! You couldn't pay me enough money to do that, and yet this young lady looked at it from a completely different angle. She said how she took pride in making the deceased look their best for the last time, and in providing that final dignity.

I use these two examples to illustrate that every one of us is unique. No one else out of seven billion people on earth has your fingerprint. Each one of us is unique with talents, natural gifts and a drive to fulfill different roles. When you look at it from this point of view, you now realize how important it is to put the right person in the right job or position.

In an earlier chapter we reviewed the recruitment part. In this chapter I want to share my experience and thoughts about HR management.

Know your people

As we mentioned in the last chapter, your first step is to describe the job and the position you would like to fill since each and every one of us is different. Each one of us is gifted in a specific field with a disposition for a particular task or job. Some people are outgoing extroverts while others are committed introverts. Some people need to work with people and others like to work on their own. There are leaders and followers. There are those who like routine and those who like change. Some like to follow instructions and procedures while others like to have freedom and flexibility.

Assigning the right person to the right job is key to achieving consistently high-quality productivity. If we can apply the idea of passion to the work, then exceptional performance will result. This is why understanding your people well is key to putting the right people in the right job.

When I say get to know your people, I mean this. Get to understand them, take a real interest in them, and be genuine in your desire to discover the real person contained in every individual. Do you need to be a psychologist? No, not really. But you need to know the person beyond superficial knowledge. Take the time to discover people's passions and talents. Working in their area of passion will not only make them shine, but will also provide for more job fulfillment and satisfaction.

Coaching rather than managing

A good manager is like a coach. You have the experience, but you also know your players very well. You know what they can do and what they cannot do. You know what they need in terms of training and what they need in order to develop and excel. You also get to know what drives them, motivates them and turns them off. You know what encourages them and what discourages them. Equipped with this two-sided knowledge of what the job requires and what the person can give will make you a good coach and a better manager.

With limited resources, you must be able to set priorities and allocate resources. A good coach can also sell to the team the changing priorities and the need to be flexible.

Be fair but manage people differently!

A good manager, while being fair to everyone on their team, manages people differently. How?

Peter is a pretty independent guy. You can give him more room to maneuver, but John needs specific instructions, so you must stay close to him and supervise him tightly. Mary gets discouraged easily and needs frequent encouragement while Joan, who is pretty autonomous and self-motivated, needs some direction. Oliver has to follow instructions and procedures. He does well with structured work but Sandra is the opposite since she has a lot of initiative and creativity. She does not perform well under lots of instructions and procedures, but she excels through her own creativity and originality. So, Oliver excels in a structured and disciplined environment while Sandra excels in finding solutions.

Be fair to all your people, but a one-size-fits-all approach does not work with those who have diverse skills and natural talents!

Clear expectations and specific objectives

A good manager takes the time to lay out clear expectations and makes it obvious what needs to be done. It shouldn't come across like a guessing game. Explain clearly what must be done and when, so employees have no doubt about what is an excellent outcome, a good outcome, a mediocre outcome and an unacceptable outcome.

If you set objectives, it's better to set them with your employee. Take the time to discuss the objective(s), how you arrived at them, and what went into establishing them. If objectives are set jointly, there is better engagement and buy-in. Employees always show a higher commitment with this cooperative approach.

Make sure you also define the individual and team objectives. Usually, there aren't only individual objectives, but team objectives that require the pulling together of corporate resources.

Resolving conflicts

When conflicts arise between team members, between departments or between you and an employee, be quick to sit down and discuss the issue at hand and then seek a solution. Do not procrastinate and do not wait for the problem to grow. Many managers think problems will go away with time. In 95% of the cases, problems do not go away. In fact, they get bigger if not resolved quickly and efficiently.

Some problems are obvious and visible, while others are hidden or just beneath the surface. It doesn't matter if a problem is visible or hidden. You must get in there and resolve it. Nobody likes conflicts and nobody likes confrontations, but they are part of the management job. A manager who cannot confront or who shies away from confrontation is an ineffective one.

Conducting performance reviews

Conducting a minimum of one performance review after 60 days for new employees and at least one annual review is important. Performance reviews help establish two-way communication in a formal manner. While the day-to-day interaction between manager and employee will contribute to good communication, the performance review is a formal tool to let the employee know what kind of a job they are doing and what needs to be done for the future. Most importantly, it gives the employee the opportunity to provide formal feedback, offer suggestions or bring up other issues that may hinder performance.

A performance review does not need to be elaborate or detailed. Its complexity will depend on the position, but suffice to say that the performance review process is key to good healthy management. Good management equals good performance.

Long-term career planning

It is good to discuss long-term career planning with employees by charting a potential career path and what needs to be done to achieve it. Career planning helps improve employee loyalty, commitment and, most importantly, employee engagement. Good career planning will include additional training that is needed and/or specific missions to develop the employee's skills and experience. Long-term career planning is usually done jointly, and not only between manager and employee. It is shared between senior managers so that the process will include interdepartmental promotion and transfers between departments, divisions or companies that comprise the group.

When you have a good career-planning process in your company, succession planning becomes easier and promotions follow a set career path. Effective succession planning contributes to such benefits as higher productivity, high-quality products and services, greater employee engagement, high loyalty, fewer interruptions and improved customer satisfaction.

Positioning the team through your organizational structure

I like clear organizational structure that shows who reports to whom, and who is responsible for what. I like to separate between solid lines of reporting and dotted lines of reporting. You may have guessed that I prefer solid lines, but I can live with dotted lines when it is appropriate. Dotted lines are sometimes useful and necessary, but when you have dotted lines, which would be the case for persons with more than one official boss, performance reviews become extremely important. And good communication between the two bosses becomes paramount.

Positioning your team through the organizational structure allows you to have good alignment between the objectives of the company and the resources. Think of a sports coach who is positioning the team for an important game. The coach will position the team after taking into consideration many factors including the strengths and weaknesses, and not only of their team, but of the opposing team.

Consider the following example: If you have the international sales manager report to the general sales manager or the president, it will send a different message to the team. If you have the HR manager reporting directly to the president or the CFO, it will send a different message as well.

Organizational structure should also change according to the business situation. For example, is the company seeking rapid growth, stability or consolidation? Is it positioned for "attack" or "defense" or "consolidation"? All these things must be taken into account.

Terminations

Termination is a delicate subject, but no chapter on human resources would be complete without covering terminations. When performance is sub-par, and training and coaching doesn't work, there is no other option but to terminate employment. Termination should never be a surprise to the employee. It should be the last step in a process of disciplinary actions.

Unless you are Donald Trump, terminating employees is one of the toughest things you have to do. Here are a few tips to ensure that the process is smooth, the individual maintains his or her dignity, and your company is at a low risk of getting sued for wrongful dismissal.

Unless you are firing someone for gross misconduct, you should have adequate documentation to justify the termination. As mentioned earlier, terminating employment for poor performance should never come as a surprise to the employee. Make sure you have a record of written documentation with adequate warnings along the way. If you have not been doing this, consider giving a warning along with specific objectives and timelines for improved performance before moving to termination.

The value of preparation cannot be understated. Have all your documentation, along with the necessary paperwork, ready for the meeting. Practice what you are going to say. Be prepared for a variety of reactions. The more prepared you are, the better it is. Make sure you follow employment standards laws in your jurisdiction. This is important when determining if a severance package will be paid out and what the legal procedures may be. Severance payment will differ from country to country, from state to state, and from province to province. I always recommend that you pay a little more than what is prescribed by law. This is not only for the benefit of the terminated employee, but it should be company policy.

In all cases, encourage the person to sign a release document. Have legal counsel review all documents so you are mitigating any potential risk of legal action. Schedule your meeting early in the day and early in the week. This gives the person time to absorb the news, make contacts and begin restructuring their time, rather than having to stew about their firing over the weekend.

I also recommend that you have someone in the room with you. If you are not a human resources practitioner, have HR involved. Treat the person who is being let go with kindness and respect, and ensure him or her of absolute confidentiality. No matter what the reaction, the person will likely be feeling vulnerable. Talk about specific behaviors that led to the termination and not inherent personality characteristics of the individual.

Be compassionate, but firm and honest. Be brief; prolonging the meeting allows employees to believe that they are in a negotiation. Finally, offer words of encouragement and always thank the person for their service.

Union or no union?

In general, managers prefer to manage non-unionized employees, and that is understandable for obvious reasons. Whether you are in a unionized or non-unionized environment, you must respect employees, treat people fairly and manage your team with excellence. These are the key ingredients for successful HR management. A non-unionized environment provides more flexibility, but a good manager will have good results in both environments.

In a unionized labor environment, focus on working together and underline the need for teamwork. Common objectives, common destiny and common rewards are the key to success. Never allow the "us vs. them" mentality to set in.

A word about innovation and employee engagement

While we're still on the chapter of managing people, I would like to share my opinion on the topics of "innovation" and "employee engagement," which are hot themes these days. Big theories abound about how to bring innovation back into the organization and how to promote employee engagement.

I don't believe you can *manufacture* innovation. Innovation or the process of innovating, which may involve creating a new product, finding a new solution or inventing a creative new way of doing something, is sparked by creativity and inspiration. It can't be switched on or off. Innovation happens when people are creative, use their imagination or are inspired. I may oversimplify this, but innovation largely depends on how the leaders of the organization behave.

A strong leader who knows how to assign every person to their right place, how to create a team that wants to succeed and how to pursue a specific vision and common goal will facilitate innovation. When people work in their area of passion and are supported, respected and properly led, the outcome will contain innovation.

Of course, some actions can promote innovation such as financial support, technical resources and relevant technology, but in the fundamental sense people innovate when they are relaxed, committed, engaged and passionate about what they do.

Take musicians who excel when they improvise, as opposed to those who excel only when they read music. These are two very different scenarios.

If leaders don't create an environment that promotes creativity, allows you to try new ways and encourages novelty and improvement, there will not be any innovation. And employee engagement will not occur. Good leaders promote the achievement of corporate objectives and care for their people. This is important. See my favorite quote at the beginning of this chapter by John C. Maxwell: "People never care how much you know until they know how much you care." Indeed, if leaders promote and contribute "life balance" in their organization, and do a good job as managers and leaders, then employee engagement will reach new highs.

In other words, you cannot legislate it. You have to believe it and live it!

CHAPTER 9

SALES MANAGEMENT

"Make a customer not a sale."
— Katherine Barchetti

Maverick Leadership© would not be complete without a chapter dedicated to sales management. Over the last 20 years, I have had more than 300 consulting assignments, and at least half of them involved sales and sales-related mandates.

Building sales and taking a company to the next level — beyond the stage of initial growth — is a big challenge for small and medium-size businesses.

Building a brand with a limited budget and resources is indeed a great test for any business. The definition of small and medium-size businesses may differ depending on where you are, but it's fair to say that small and medium-size businesses face challenges when they try to move from a sales force of two or three people to ten or more.

Many successful general managers and entrepreneurs get stuck with issues that end up hindering the continued growth of their top line. Let's get these out of the way before we address some really good recommendations for sales growth. Here are the three main ones:

1) Promoting your best salesperson to sales manager

The first pitfall is to promote the best salesperson to the position of sales manager without doing your homework. Your best salesperson may be the right candidate for the position if they have the right ingredients, but the promotion should not be automatic or a foregone conclusion.

It is true that almost all good sales managers started as salespeople, but it's also true that not all good salespeople make good sales managers.

Today many HR tests exist that analyze a person's gifts, strengths and character traits. One of my personal favorites is the Birkman Method©, which identifies a person's passions, behaviors, motivations and interests. It is a very powerful tool and a good one to use when making people decisions involving recruitment or promotions.

Salespeople need to be persuasive and disciplined in their activities since they are responsible for their own work and results. Sales managers should have these traits as well, but they must also be good managers and team builders. They are responsible for team results, and not only individual results. These two positions require different sets of skills.

2) Compensation

The second pitfall is when the compensation package of your sales force becomes out of line and outdated. Your sales compensation package was initially designed to get sales from point A to point B. While it was effective in getting the company to point B, it may not be the right compensation plan for getting sales from point B to point C.

For example, if your star salesperson John is now earning big bucks for what seems to be little work, it may not be his fault. If Jane, your star key account manager, now earns more than the president, it may not be her fault. In fact, Jane must have greatly exceeded the top of her sales target and that's good. You want to have lots of Janes on your team, but it is the compensation plan that must be tweaked — not Jane!

HR compensation experts can be engaged for advice. You do not need to reinvent the wheel, but you do want to retain John and Jane, and remunerate them well. You also want to grow the business in a healthy manner. A good compensation plan can achieve all three objectives.

3) Sales and marketing plan

Do you have an up-to-date sales and marketing plan? If not, then you should prepare one.

What is a sales and marketing plan? It is a document that spells out where you are in sales, where you want to be and how to get there. It is similar to a strategic plan but deals with sales and marketing subjects rather than the entire company.

A sales and marketing plan does not have to be a huge document. The size and complexity depends on the size and complexity of your company. Your sales and marketing plan should include your industry and outline such things as sales, competition, customer analysis, sales and marketing objectives, product and service strategies, pricing, advertising and promotions, resource requirements, compensation, sales process and sales training. It may sound complicated, but it really isn't. A good sales and marketing plan will keep you focused and help you stay on course.

You can't separate sales from marketing, or marketing from sales. They are two brothers and must work hand in hand to grow your business in a healthy, steady manner. In general, marketing is more strategic and sales more tactical, hence the close working relationship between the two to make your business perform well for the short, medium and long term.

These three issues may all be pretty basic, but they are key to your future success if you want to grow sales in a healthy manner and build a strong brand.

With these three major pitfalls behind us, let me now share two very important lists.

The first list spells out **things that should be present in your sales department**. These are key things that will contribute to your success. If you don't have them, you need to implement them.

The second list contains **things that hinder your progress and your sales growth**. If any of these things exist in your company, then you need to take action. In other words, these are the warning signs of a demoralized and dysfunctional sales department.

The "TO DO" sales list

1) New clients

Does your company have a healthy flow of new clients every month? And every year? Or do your sales come from the same clients you acquired in the past? A constant flow of new clients is the lifeblood of any business.

2) Repeat clients

Do your clients come back for more? How is repeat business? A healthy and growing business should generate most of its sales and revenues from existing clients. This is not a contradiction of my first point. You need a good balance between new and existing clients. Depending on one or the other is not healthy for the long term.

3) Sales objectives

Do you have sales objectives for your sales manager and your sales force? Does the sales department achieve or exceed its sales objectives? Constantly missing sales objectives is a de-motivator and a big warning sign of fatigue. Objectives should be established jointly between the salesperson and their manager. And sales objectives should be backed by a yearly sales plan. For an example of a sales plan, see the appendix at the end of this book.

4) Testimonials and customer/prospect survey

Do your clients write testimonials for you? Do your salespeople ask for testimonials? It is better to have clients praise you and say how good your products and services than you saying these things yourself. But, if you don't ask for testimonials, how will you get them? Every salesperson should receive at least one or two testimonials per month. They should be in groups, included on your website and used in your sales handout material.

I also recommend that you ask loyal and satisfied clients to participate in short testimonial videos no more than one to two minutes long. In these videos they should say why you are different and what you bring to the table that others don't. These videos can be very effective on your website, at trade shows and in supporting your sales materials, as well as in your promotion and advertising campaigns.

I will also include in this section on testimonials the need to conduct periodic customer surveys. Customer surveys conducted via the Internet, telephone or mail allow you to gather feedback in a uniform, independent and professional manner. It's not like feedback obtained one-on-one by your salespeople, employees or managers.

Today's technology makes conducting a customer survey affordable and very doable. The use of specialized services such as SurveyMonkey.com and SoGoSurvey.com, to cite two, offer exceptional tools for conducting effective surveys. They also provide a comprehensive set of analytical tools that analyze, tabulate, report, present and summarize survey results.

An annual survey can provide excellent feedback for your sales and marketing activities, and highlight opportunities, challenges and threats. Comparing your annual surveys over a period of time also brings to light important trends in your business in terms of customer satisfaction, feedback, products and service usage, service effectiveness, etc.

5) Referrals and sales leads

Do your salespeople get referrals from clients and sales leads from their business network? Referrals are the best way to get new clients. It is very dangerous to have no referrals. Happy customers are pleased to refer others because they want to share the good news!

No referrals can mean one of two things: (a) clients are not comfortable recommending your company, or (b) your salespeople are not asking for referrals. Ask your salespeople to approach existing customers for referrals. Word of mouth is one of the best tools for acquiring new customers.

6) Case studies

Case studies that show the "before and after" effect are also an effective sales tool (i.e., how your products and services benefit your clients). Case studies are very effective when you need to convince skeptical prospects about the validity and value of your products and services. Case studies backed by numbers and factual data offer strong evidence of what you can do for clients. The use of case studies has been documented to be one of the most convincing arguments in the sales process and should be obtained regularly by your salespeople. Your website and your sales handout material should contain numerous case studies that can be used to illustrate circumstances and challenges facing your customers.

7) Celebrations and recognition

Does your sales department and your company celebrate wins? Celebrating special achievements by individual employees and by salespeople in particular helps keep the momentum positive and the troops motivated. Celebration can be as small as a brief speech or presentation, a pizza lunch, or a special lunch at a good restaurant where you offer gift certificates.

During my long career at the D&B Nielsen Group, I don't remember a single month that went by without one or two celebrations. For a celebration to be successful, it must be genuine. But don't be discouraged if not all staff enjoy these celebrations: Some may never get involved, but most of them will.

Use your imagination when you reward employees. For example, adding a limo service to a dinner for two may increase the cost, but it will always be remembered as a special occasion. I once rented a red Ferrari for a weekend for a sales manager in France. I knew that he loved Ferraris. He and all the staff will forever remember that reward (never mind that the car insurance for the weekend cost more than the rental fees!). Another side benefit of the Ferrari reward was that our CFO visited a church on Sunday to light candles; he was praying that nothing would happen to the Ferrari.

Money is always appreciated, but monetary rewards are usually forgotten over time while other forms of recognition will be long remembered by the recipient and by all the team members. People appreciate and want recognition and acknowledgment of their contribution.

8) Key customer and prospect information (KCPI)

You should identify key customers and key prospects, and keep a comprehensive file on them. The file should be prepared by salespeople. They may need help for entering the initial information, but it is their responsibility to maintain their KCPIs and keep them up to date.

The KCPI file will contain comprehensive intelligence on the key customers and prospects. This information will include key people, identified needs, competitive intelligence, yearly business plans, newspaper clippings, financial statements, extracts from annual reports, credit reports and other important customer information. KCPI should be reviewed at least twice a year by management. For a sample of a KCPI file, please refer to the appendix. You will find two sample templates of the KCPI — a long version and a short version. You can customize these documents to fit your needs and change the content of the KCPI to better match or to cover the specifics of your product(s)/service(s). These KCPI files and the MS Outlook system for your daily and weekly communication with customers will allow you to have a very good CRM system (customer relationship management).

CRM is an approach to managing a company's interactions with current and future customers. It involves using technology to organize, automate and synchronize sales, marketing, customer service and technical support. You can purchase a specific CRM system or use existing standard software applications. A combination of the KCPI, MS Outlook, and MS Excel is sufficient for most sales needs.

It is worth mentioning that the initial loading or data entry of KCPI can be done by part-time students or interns who are hired specifically to load all key clients and prospects information into a KCPI database. Updates can then be done by the sales force.

9) Sales training

Does your company have a budget for training? And is there a specific budget for sales training? Companies often have initial training for new employees and for new salespersons, but little follow-up training. New employee training is a must, but follow-through training is even more important because it will address specific areas that need training. Follow-through training can be customized and personalized.

Sales training is helpful for salespeople, but other training may be even more beneficial. I suggest telephone training that includes how to best use the telephone, how to leave effective voice mail/messages, how to write and manage emails and so on. Of course, face-to-face sales training is important, but in today's marketplace effective use of telephone, texting, MS Outlook and emails may be just as important.

Finally, do you have a sales process (also called sales cycle) for your sales force to use as a guideline? Your sales process may differ by sales channel. For example, telesales involves a different process than selling in the field. The key account managers may have a different one, too. Distributors or re-sellers (if you have them) may also have a different sales process. Without taking anything away from the initiative and creativity of your salespeople, you would be wise to have a well-defined sales process as a good benchmark.

Time and time again, successful salespeople attribute their success to their sales process or to their sales activities, rather than a "magic" sales touch. The magic sales touch is definitely needed, but it's the discipline of the sales process that brings exceptional results and helps maintain them. For a sample sales process, please refer to the appendix.

Still on the subject of training, I want to bring to your attention the need to coach top performers, as well as lower performers. All too often, sales managers spend too much time with their low performers and leave their top performers with little or no coaching.

You can disagree with me, but I recommend spending half of your energy, time and focus on **coaching and developing your best performers**, taking them to higher levels. How do you do that? First, by treating them as valuable members of the team and showing your appreciation. Second, by learning their personal goals and career aspirations so you can develop their professional skills and get them promoted. Offer them advanced training and various other courses, as well as continuing education seminars. This will build their professional skills and prepare them for higher levels of responsibility and for greater contributions and results. Identify their weaknesses and let them find alternative ways to rectify those weaknesses, but most importantly hone in on their strengths and get those strengths developed because these strengths will take them to a higher level.

10) Customer profitability

Do you track profitability by customer? Most companies analyze and classify customers by sales or revenues. The smart ones further analyze and classify their customers by profitability or gross profit and gross margin. This is very important and revealing, especially when large customers benefit from discounts or special pricing or what is called negotiated "freebies." If salespeople have authority to negotiate special prices and discounts, then it is worthwhile to consider a sales commission based on gross profit rather than strictly on sales volume.

Gross profit is usually calculated by subtracting the cost of goods sold (or direct costs) from your sales, while gross margin is obtained by dividing your gross profit by sales and then multiplying the result by 100. Your gross margin is expressed as a percentage of sales.

The "NOT TO DO" sales list

1) Missed sales objectives

Failure to achieve sales objectives or sales quotas is frustrating and may cause underperforming salespeople to lose their self-confidence. You must understand the reasons for the missed numbers: Are the quotas realistic? Do they reflect market realities? Is sales training needed? You and your salespeople should set sales objectives together and have a specific plan for achieving the objectives. Achieving and exceeding sales objectives is a powerful motivator and team builder.

2) Grumbling

People grumble when they are frustrated. Look for signs of frustration when people criticize each other, criticize the system or keep using the "us-and-them" vocabulary. Keep your ears to the ground and get to know the source of the discontent. What needs of the salespeople are not addressed? When you find out, review the actions that can bring effective solutions to these needs. Bring enthusiasm and the spirit of team play back into the sales group.

3) Rules and more rules

If the sales department has lots of rules and there is a manual of what to do for almost every situation, and a deadline for many things, you may want to investigate the need for these rules and regulations. Successful salespeople are usually creative, outspoken and extroverts. And they love freedom. Excessive rules may reveal underground issues that need to be addressed. I understand the importance of rules and regulations, but a disproportionate number of rules can suffocate people, hinder their productivity and lower morale.

Managers often introduce rules, regulations and internal policies in order to change people's behavior. Rules and regulations do indeed change people's behavior, but they change them only on the surface. I prefer a more professional style of management where people use their common sense and their own initiative to perform their work and create results. What I mean is that I set the bar of professionalism high so people are pulled up through their own initiative and professional conduct, as opposed to being pulled down through rules and regulations. My experience also shows that when you have lots of rules and regulations, there is more discussion and arguing about these things and less time spent on the work and the results that you want. Reaching a balance between rules on one side and autonomy and creativity on the other side is difficult and delicate. It requires strong leadership, but the rewards are worth it.

4) **Excessive complaints**

Complaints by salespeople to the HR manager may be an indication of frustration with management or with co-workers. This creates an unhealthy work environment. Find out what the root of these complaints are, and then remove any obstacles to sales performance and productivity. Genuine complaints should be handled and resolved quickly and fairly. Never leave a complaint lingering unresolved.

5) **Cross-departmental blaming**

The conflict between the sales department and the operations department is a well-known dynamic. So is the hidden criticism between the salespeople and the accounting people. Don't accept these stereotypical relationships as normal and par for the course. Get all the people involved and promote a one-team spirit.

Without customers and sales, we have no business. And without effective collections and accurate accounting, we have no profits. And with no profit, we have no business. I often use the example of a boat. We are in a boat, and making a hole on your side of the boat is destructive to everyone on the boat. It doesn't matter where the hole is. In another example, we are like a sports team; individual performance is wonderful, but we win or lose collectively.

As you will note, the **TO DO** sales list contains ten subjects and the **NOT TO DO** sales list contains only five items. Don't mix them up!

CHAPTER 10

THE LOW-HANGING FRUITS IN YOUR PRICING SYSTEM

> "Price is what you pay. Value is what you get."
> — Warren Buffett

Finding pricing opportunities is similar to a gold miner striking gold. Price increases add directly to the bottom line because there is usually no corresponding increase of costs, provided there is no reduced volume of sales because of the price increase.

Price increases that are accepted by customers indicate that customers are fully satisfied with your product and service and don't want to change their purchasing behavior. They see value in your product and service. The extra revenues generated are a direct contributor to increased profitability.

In this chapter we will handle in detail pricing opportunities and how to discover the gold hidden in your pricing system.

Here is what I discovered through many assignments over my career in Canada and around the world. In the vast majority of cases, managers already knew what was wrong with their companies. Unfortunately, there was usually no agreement on the solutions, no focus and no objectives to address the issues. I also found that there were no specific plans laid out and no defined milestones.

Another key obstacle is the myopic view of senior managers who were looking only at their area of responsibility. This is commonly described in business as silos. This type of approach sees managers focused on their silo rather than taking the overall corporate view and working with a true team approach. What I usually found was that, even with good intentions, leadership was overworked and incurred sleepless nights over issues that remained blurred, largely because the solutions didn't address the problem.

This situation made my search for gold easier as I would usually identify a handful of actions that had to be addressed immediately. I would then be in a position to present senior management with a set of real priorities and offer a road map that would get them on the road to success.

In most of my assignments, I would pinpoint a diagnosis after investigating key information and doing some fact finding. Invariably, the pricing system was often an area with an abundance of low-hanging fruit.

Low-hanging fruit comes quick and easy with little effort. It can lead to immediate benefits for the organization's bottom line. However, spending too much time on low-hanging fruit means we fail to see the profit that can be easily harvested with a few simple recalibrations in a company's pricing system.

Better control over price means better control over profitability

For example, let's assume you are a distributor and buy an item for $75 and then sell it for $100, resulting in a 25% gross margin ($100 selling price minus $75 cost of goods = $25 gross profit or 25% gross margin). If $22 goes to overhead, you are left with 3% of pre-tax profit ($25 gross profit minus $22 overhead cost = $3 pretax profit or a profit margin of 3%).

A $1-price increase (1%) means selling at $101, but the cost of goods remains unchanged at $75. This increases the gross margin to $26 and your pre-tax profit now becomes 4%. This increase is more than a 30% increase to your bottom-line! In this example a 1% price increase to the selling price results in a 30% increase in profitability.

If you examine the numbers in your own organization, do a trial calculation to find out what effect a 1% to 5% increase would have on your pre-tax profit. The answer often surprises clients by how much difference it can make.

Whenever I introduce a price increase as a potential subject, management invariably tells me that the market forces usually set the price and it would be suicidal to increase price. Yet, time and time again, I always find many ways to increase price.

Here is a short list of principles that could be applied to your business:

Mark-up formula is general

Most companies arrive at a mark-up percentage or a mark-up multiplier by item sold or category of items. For example, a company would multiply the cost of purchasing by a factor of 1.4 or 1.5 to arrive at the selling price. An item purchased at $10 would then sell for $14 or $15.

While this formula might have been good when the company had a limited number of items, it is probably overly simplistic when the company adds countless items to its product line and/or expands beyond its original line of products.

Examine your inventory of items and break it down into categories, and then into subcategories. Then review your mark-up for every item. In reviewing your prices, you should consider many factors such as the item cost, the estimated turns of the item (turns per year or inventory turnover), customer behavior, the competitive climate and your own gross profit objective.

This straightforward analysis may identify pockets of opportunities for increased prices (e.g., Category A is marked-up by 1.5, Category B by 1.6, Category C by 1.7 and so on). Exceptions within a category may also be made if you have exclusive items and/or items that are hard to compare with the competition.

When items are exclusive to you or hard to compare with other items on the market, you have a greater opportunity to raise the price. Again, this must be done intelligently and with balance.

Discounts

Most companies offer discounts in one form or another. Discounts can be derived from volume of purchases, type of products, type of customers and geography, just to name a few. While discounts are an effective tool to win new business, they can cut deeply into your profit if they are not well thought out and carefully implemented.

Is your sales team using discounts wisely, or are they giving discounts to all customers? Analyze your discount policy frequently and make sure the policy achieves your objectives. Similarly, track how your sales force is using discounts to win new business, while making sure that discounts are not given as part of a normal routine. Discounts should be used effectively to win business from your competitors.

Price band analysis

This analysis is designed to create a clear graph of all your pricing activity during a specific period of time. Analyzing the results and taking actions based on the results can add a few points to your gross margin.

The vertical axis represents the percentage of business sold at the particular margin listed on the horizontal axis. In our example, 15% of the business sold during the specific period was sold at 10% margin, 20% at 15%, 40% at 20% margin and so on.

Price band

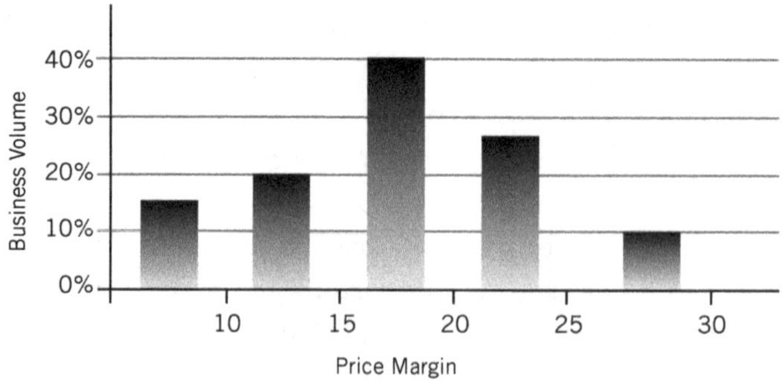

This analysis tells us that (a) 75% of the volume was sold at a margin of 20%–30% while 25% of the volume was sold at a margin of 5%–10%, and (b) the price band is quite large, between a margin of 10% and 30%.

You may want to analyze the 25% volume sold at a low margin to see if you can improve the selling price. You may also want to put forward a strategy to narrow the existing large price band. It may be difficult to increase the margin on the 25% portion of sales, but the analysis may help you find ways to increase sales of the 75% portion of the product. If you succeed in this, then you would be changing the business mix by selling more product at the higher margin, which will result in an increase of the gross margin.

Elasticity of demand

The golden economic rule of supply and demand says that demand will increase if price drops, and demand will drop when price increases. That is true for most products, but there are also markets with low elasticity of demand.

This is particularly applicable for prestige products or innovative and unique products. Check the elasticity of your product or service, and you may find opportunity for price increases.

Bundling and unbundling

As companies grow, bundling of products may occur with prices no longer assigned for each component or item. Instead, they are now assigned for the whole. A customer may then come along and ask for the price of an individual item, and during the process you may end up losing a few pricing points.

You may want to review the effect that bundling and unbundling products has on your prices by asking these questions:

- Does your product include a large amount of service?
- Should you price the product in a way that bundles the physical product with the service or do you price the product separately from the service portion?

- Do you price your product and include the transportation cost or do you price it excluding the cost of transportation?

Remember that price is the only element in the marketing mix that produces revenue; the other elements represent cost. Yet my experience clearly indicates that the vast majority of medium-sized businesses do not handle pricing properly.

The most common mistakes are that pricing becomes too cost-oriented, the price is not revised often enough to capitalize on market changes (I call them "market opportunities") and prices are set independently from the rest of the marketing strategy or package.

Here are six key steps you should consider when setting your prices:

1) Determine price objective
2) Estimate demand
3) Estimate costs
4) Analyze competitors' pricing
5) Consider price as an intrinsic element of your marketing strategy
6) Choose your pricing formula and tactic

Profit is not a dirty word, and while you don't want to fleece your customers, you want to identify pricing opportunities and take action to harvest these opportunities in order to optimize your profit.

While covering the issue of pricing, I would like to share some opinions about what not to do.

With many products, and especially with consumer packaged goods, you see the manufacturer playing with the size of the packaged product. For example, a 500-gram package of pasta is sold for $2 then what looks like the same package but weighs only 450 grams is sold for the same $2. That is a hidden 11% price increase!

In my opinion, this is unethical because most consumers/customers may not initially notice that the quantity on the package has changed. Since the reduction of the quantity was only 10%, chances are they missed it. You may think there was nothing unethical here since the package clearly states that the quantity is now 450 grams. While that is true, the intention was to trick the customer and get away with a hidden price increase. I disagree with this approach.

In a similar example, a retailer advertises a 50% off sale, but then limits the sale to very few items in the store. Thus, the 50% off sale was just a gimmick to get consumers in the store.

Another common tactic is to price an item with an exorbitant price for a couple of days (nobody bought at that price) and then have it 50% off. This is called "dress it before you discount it." Such pricing tactics are not what I am talking about in this chapter, and I recommend staying away from these gimmicky tactics.

Low-hanging fruit strategies that harvest accessible profits quickly and easily must include the respect and appreciation of the customer at the very core.

CHAPTER 11

THE OLIVE PRINCIPLE

Managing Costs

"Productivity is never an accident,
it's the result of a commitment to excellence,
intelligent planning and focused effort."
— Paul Meyer

In this chapter I will share some ideas, concepts and suggestions about cost management. It's a fundamental building block that is more important than you think. Keep in mind that business knowledge, whether basic or advanced, is powerful only when applied. What determines your business performance is executing the concept, not only the simplicity, complexity or innovative ideas that are associated with it. Taking action on sound fundamental principles is the key to any successful project.

What business are you in?

If cost leadership is crucial to your bottom line and to your very survival, you must constantly reengineer your costs and watch every penny like a hawk.

If you are in a niche business, cost is certainly important to your bottom line, but you may be able to get away with a few inefficiencies.

Another big influencer in your success is who your competitors are and how they compete. Take a look at your competitors to see if they are huge organizations or smaller outfits. Competing with large players requires different skills than competing with smaller players.

Whether you have a big or small margin, you need to watch costs and manage overall productivity in order to optimize your bottom line and maintain leadership in a competitive marketplace.

Your organization's success depends primarily on what you do and how you serve your customers. For example, if your competitor is Wal-Mart, which is known for low prices, you will have a very difficult time competing on pricing. Wal-Mart is known for efficient procurement, exceptional logistics and overall cost efficiency.

So if you want to compete with Wal-Mart, you must compete on a differentiation strategy. What's that? A differentiation strategy, rather than a "me too" strategy, is the best strategy for competing against a low-price competitor. It means advertising that you are better, faster, nicer or more flexible — whatever your differentiating factor is from Wal-Mart. Staying away from price comparison could be a more effective approach because Wal-Mart would probably beat most competitors in a price-comparison campaign.

That being said, here are some examples where even mighty Wal-Mart had setbacks when invading new markets. A few years ago, in an effort to invade Europe, Wal-Mart chose to first attack the German market, which is not the traditional way to penetrate Europe. They failed and had to exit. Local competitors designed a solid strategy and pricing tactics that did not allow Wal-Mart to make headway in the local market.

Another time, their Sam's Club division tried to invade Canada, but found a fierce competitor in Costco, which was not about to roll over, and Sam's Club had to retreat. Finally, there is Target, which participated in the Canadian market from 2013–2015 with 133 stores. But they had to retreat when sales did not pick up and existing competitors ferociously defended their market share. Target exited after losing and writing off well over $1 billion in investment and losses.

These examples illustrate the importance of having the right strategy and knowing if you will compete on the basis of "me too" or "differentiation." Cost will play a big part in your strategy.

Is it a cost or an investment?

Many entrepreneurs don't make a distinction between an expense and an investment. Your accountant or bookkeeper may not have asked how you want particular items treated. Don't wait for them to ask. Instead, take the initiative by sharing what you are doing with them. Expenses directed to developing new products, new services, or new processes can all be classified as research and development (R&D). That means they may qualify to be capitalized rather than expensed.

Let's assume you are producing three types of widgets: A, B and C. Your total sales were $100 and your costs $80. So your profit is $20. This seems straightforward. But baked into the $80 of costs were $10 dedicated to experimentation and to building a new and improved widget D. Your costs then, were really only $ 70, and $ 10 would be better classified as R&D. You may still want to throw the $ 10 into your regular cost base, but be clear on what the operating expenses are, how many dollars went to R&D and what the actual profit is. A clear differentiation is needed.

This is very important for CEOs and especially for those who are constantly experimenting and trying new initiatives. R&D is good, but it must be controlled. Unless you happen to have a fantastic profit margin that allows unlimited resources for R&D, you must plan your R&D investments in advance or run the risk of overinvesting and hurting your bottom line.

Some big corporations may have the opposite problem. In their desire to maximize profit, they don't allow for sufficient R&D investment at the local business unit. This may short-change healthy growth in the future. Unless there is great strategic need, neither of these extremes is desired.

You should seek a balance between short-term performance and long-term performance. Many companies allocate a certain percentage of sales to R&D so they can come up with new products and services that help sustain their performance over time.

In a nutshell:

a) Don't mix expense and investment in your mind and in the books.
b) Determine how much you want to invest in R&D ahead of time.

Compare your costs against internal and external benchmarks

Most businesspeople compare their costs internally. The most common comparisons are year-over-year and quarterly. This is good, but don't stop there. You should also compare your costs against external benchmarks. Can you compare costs against competitors or against big public companies in your industry? If not, you may want to check out general statistics offered by third parties.

In Canada, Revenue Canada and Statistics Canada offer excellent statistics that can be used for benchmarking. In the United States, the IRS and industry associations are also good sources. These are very helpful. Ask yourself: How am I doing on cost issues vs. others in my industry, and what is my trend? Am I gaining or losing ground? First Research (FirstResearch.com) provides concise industry profiles that can be used to effectively benchmark certain costs.

Sales-absorption analysis

Sales-absorption analysis sounds intimidating, but is really straightforward. Most accountants provide their clients with this analysis on their P&L. Usually this reads as follows: Look at total sales as 100% with each cost item a percentage of the 100%. So the cost of goods sold may be 60%, and within that 60% are raw materials at 30%, labor at 20% and factory overhead at 10%. The gross margin is 40%. This is great, but if you have more than one product or service, dumping all the costs into one big bucket doesn't provide much insight. Prepare a separate P&L by product (e.g., Product A has a gross margin of 40%, Product B 60% and Product C 15%). While their mix resulted in an overall gross margin of 40%, the separate profitability analysis by product revealed that Product B was the real star that compensated for the low margin of product C. Now you can work on the costs of Product C to improve your overall profitability.

You will always get surprises when you separate cost calculations using elements relevant to the business such as product line, service components, revenue streams and geography. When you do this, you will find that the numbers look different, and many opportunities reveal themselves, especially in the area of cost management.

It is imperative to know the profitability of each product and service, and to analyze the various cost components over several years to identify positive and negative trends. And if you can track the cost of raw materials, you will be able to manage your purchases better and manage costs more effectively.

Variable costs and fixed costs

This is classic, but it bears reminding. Variable costs go up and down with your revenues vs. fixed costs, which choke you when revenues go down. Variable costs give you extra flexibility and allow you better protection of your margin. Even when fixed costs may appear lower, it's best to evaluate well before you pick the route of fixed costs. Flexibility is of great benefit in today's fast-paced business environment.

Outsourcing

Concentrate on what you do best, and evaluate the advantages of outsourcing those functions and activities which external vendors can do more efficiently. When you evaluate these opportunities, make sure the evaluation is carried out by a knowledgeable party who possesses experience and business acumen. It's also important to use an independent party who can see things objectively. Don't ask the person in charge to conduct the evaluation because there is an obvious conflict of interest. Of course, they should be involved in the process, but they should not be the decision maker (some exceptions may apply here).

I am not for or against outsourcing since I think outsourcing can be an excellent solution in many situations, but it has to be carried out carefully. Generally speaking, outsourcing is done to seek savings or better costs. While this is great, you must be sure you don't lose benefits that don't compensate for the savings.

For example, you can outsource customer service to an external organization at a much lower cost, but if the outsourcing leads to customer dissatisfaction and a loss of customers, it has clearly backfired and incurred more cost than savings for you in the long term. It could also harm your organization's reputation. This is too high a price to pay.

Let's say you outsource the manufacture of certain parts to save money only to discover that you must order these parts far in advance. Or maybe the minimum quantities are so large now that your inventory shoots up significantly. You find that your savings on one side have created extra costs elsewhere, causing the bottom line to remain materially unchanged.

I remember this story. An appliance manufacturer could not ship its finished appliances because someone in the organization outsourced the printing of the owner's manual to a printer in a third-world country, and the manuals were stuck on a boat in the middle of the ocean! A $2 manual was holding up delivery of a $1,000 appliance.

Here's another one. A purchasing manager who tried to save a fraction of a cent changed suppliers for his shopping bags, but later discovered that the new, cheaper bags were not as resilient as the original ones. Customers were irate when the bags broke and their purchases ended up all over the parking lot. That caused the people in customer service and the cashiers to double-bag, which not only eliminated the savings but resulted in slower service at the cashier!

These horror stories on cost saving gone wrong illustrate two important points:

First, it is true that costs should be managed, but they must be managed intelligently and not in a vacuum. Second, purchasing managers should be encouraged to search for new vendors with alternative costs, but must work hand-in-hand with the managers on the frontline. They must work together as a team to improve the bottom line, but not at the expense of other elements of the business such as customer satisfaction, employee productivity and quality measures.

Here are some key questions to consider before you outsource:

1) Does outsourcing help only in the short term or does it also contribute to the long term?
2) Does the outsourcing process give you better or worse flexibility?
3) Does the outsourcing affect customer satisfaction?

4) Do the reduced costs on one side of your business result in increased costs somewhere else? Are there net savings?
5) Have you checked the reliability of the outsourced company? And can they be trusted with confidential information, processes and know-how? By outsourcing, are you going to create a new competitor?

Barter

Another manner with similarities to outsourcing is working with vendors and suppliers on a barter basis (i.e., exchanging products and services of equal value without the traditional buy-and-sell commercial activity). Barter is simply a system of exchanging goods and services directly for other goods and services without using money as a medium.

For example, I give you advertising in exchange for office desks. I give you reduced pricing in my hotels (during low-occupancy periods) in exchange for reduced pricing for renovation work (during your slow construction period). The barter system, as you may imagine, has such limitations as evaluating the exchange to be of similar value and the potential effect on timing.

On the other hand, if what I have can be exchanged for what you have, barter can be very effective. I'll give you an example from my experience in Brazil. The company I managed produced credit reports and, as you know, Brazil is a very large country. Our resources for investigation and data gathering for reports in southern Brazil were very efficient, but not in northern Brazil.

Historically, the good profits made on the sale of southern credit reports compensated for losses sustained in producing credit reports for northern Brazil. I wanted to make a decent profit on both sides and not have one side subsidize the other.

With the help of my team, we identified a competitor who had almost exactly the same problem, but in reverse. He efficiently produced credit reports covering northern Brazil, but was inefficient in southern Brazil. We agreed to make an alliance: we would use him for inquiries of credit reports in northern Brazil, and he would use us for inquiries for credit reports in southern Brazil. Best of all, we would use a barter system and exchange one credit report for one credit report exchanged during the month; we would pay only for the net excess volume.

During a certain month we would purchase 200 reports and he would purchase 180 reports. So he would invoice me for only the positive difference of 20 reports. Next month, the volumes may be in my favor, and so on. We would only invoice the net difference each month. You can imagine what this simple bartering system did to my profitability; almost overnight it allowed me to reduce costs on all my credit-report production for northern Brazil, making this profitable and helping me keep the total profitability of my credit reports produced in southern Brazil. He had the same result. It was a win-win agreement.

While this example may be described as too good to be true, and it was, the point I am trying to make is this: Be open to various ways of managing costs and improving your profitability. Use all the tools at your disposal to manage your bottom line intelligently.

Purchasing

Most companies go shopping for the best value when selecting a new supplier. This is great, but what about current suppliers? This area needs constant review. You must keep your suppliers in check to ensure that you receive the best value.

I refer not only to price but also to the overall value of the relationship (e.g., quality, service, responsiveness, reliability, etc.). It is essential to keep up to date with your key suppliers. How big are they? Who owns them? What is their strategy? How are they doing?

Make sure you know how important you are to them as a customer. Let's assume that you purchase $100,000 of a product from Supplier A and $100,000 from Supplier B. It would be good to know that Supplier A has annual sales of $ 7 million and Supplier B has annual sales of $700,000. No doubt, you are important to A, but you are extremely important to B. Your leverage with B is significantly stronger.

Another rule of thumb in purchasing is to buy from someone who is hungry for your business. If you have to stand in line and take a number or be put on hold indefinitely when you call, you may want to do more research and find someone who is hungrier for your business.

At the end of this chapter is a section that deals with tools for the purchasing manager.

Productivity measures

Productivity measures tend to be forgotten by small, medium and large businesses alike. Here are some useful ratios that can help you manage your productivity: sales per employee (annual sales / number of full time equivalent), profit per employee (net profit / number of full time equivalent), average compensation per employee (total salary, wages and benefits / number of full time equivalent), units per employee (number of units produced / number of employees), sales order per salesperson (sales orders / salespeople), customers per sales representative (number of active customers / salespeople), just to name a few. Compute the ratios and compare them over an extended period of time to evaluate your trend and determine if your productivity is improving, deteriorating or flat.

Once these statistics are maintained, it is easier to figure out your productivity, to track it and to improve it. Make sure that productivity gains are an objective for every single employee in every level of the organization, regardless of rank or title. Productivity is not a subject to be addressed once a year. Productivity improvement is an ongoing process that needs constant attention.

It is a mindset

So what about the olive? And why is this chapter called "The Olive Principle"? An airline had profitability problems and decided to go after cost reductions. It started by questioning every cost item.

If we took the olive out of the salad in each passenger dinner, would this make a difference to customer satisfaction? The answer was obviously no. So, if we took away the olive, we would save X amount of a cent multiplied by X number of dinners served per month multiplied by 12 months. Removing an olive from the salad resulted in a decent saving when accumulated over a 12-month period. Result? It was agreed to remove the olive from the salad.

Next under scrutiny was the small package of cheese, followed by the strawberry in the fruit salad. This process continued into other areas such as the gold buttons on the captain's uniform and the lining in flight attendants' hats, and then asking if the hat was needed at all.

At first, an organization may become giddy with cost-cutting, but then it can become difficult to stop. For example, can you afford to cut back on maintenance if it affects safety? Ensure that cost-cutting measures are part of an overall plan and a cohesive strategy. If not, this can become a dangerous slippery slope.

The moral of the story of the airline removing the olive from the salad — and the crux of the Olive Principle — is that the olive itself does not provide customer satisfaction, but it does add to the overall value of the airline service. Don't nickel-and-dime your customer because they will nickel-and-dime you, too.

Here is one of my favorite illustrations about this point:

Let's assume I invite you to dinner in my home. You see that the dining room table has a nicely pressed tablecloth, each guest has a cloth napkin beside their well-laid plate and cutlery, there is a lit candle on the table, a small vase with a fresh rose in it, the room is clean and light music plays in the background. You are impressed with everything before you even have anything to eat.

Can you tell me which items impressed you? And how much each thing impressed you? You probably could not measure what each item adds to the ambiance, but each item does contribute to the attractive presentation, positive atmosphere and overall impression of the dinner experience.

In the same way, when dealing with cost reduction, don't just look at individual cost per item, but evaluate the overall effect and then look at your productivity. Don't focus only on the components and individual items. Ensure that you look at the overall value your customers are getting.

In my airline example, it's better to find a better olive supplier or caterer than to get rid of the olive. Focus and manage productivity rather than costs per se. Look at cost savings intelligently by becoming more efficient, and not just by beating on your suppliers, nickel-and-diming customers or treating employees like robots. By managing your productivity, cost reduction will be a natural bonus.

Now, it's a different issue if the situation is a turnaround. When a company is in trouble and in dire need of a turnaround, cost-cutting and slashing expenses is the number one priority.

In a non-turnaround scenario, however, special care must be taken to ensure that cost-cutting is an exercise that improves productivity. In short, it should augment productivity, not undermine it.

It is better to have a productivity-improvement mindset than a cost-cutting mindset. Similarly, watch out for those who on one hand offer you great savings, but on the other kill your business by chasing customers away. That is counter-productive and will only sabotage your business success.

SPECIAL SUPPLEMENT

Negotiating for better purchases with reduced price

This section offers some practical ways for negotiating better prices from suppliers and/or suggestions for lowering your costs. The purpose of these suggestions is not to treat your suppliers as enemies or to constantly beat them over the head in order to lower prices. Rather, the purpose is to work with them as partners in a joint effort for success. The more you succeed, the more they should succeed. Partnering with your suppliers is a sure way to be more successful since you are working with them as one team for a win-win relationship. Now let's take a look at some important points when building this type of relationship with your suppliers:

Comparing prices: Let's assume you buy a certain product at $100 from Supplier A. You then locate two other competitors, B and C, who have the same quality product, and you get their quotes. When armed with lower quotes, let's say $95 and $97, you go back to A and share this information without identifying suppliers. Ask A to resubmit their best offer. Supplier A will likely submit a new quote of either $95 or $97. This means you just saved $5 or 5% on your purchases.

Diversify your sources: If possible, don't have one supplier per product. Have two or more. For example, you buy 10,000 units from supplier A for $100 each. Then you identify two more suppliers and ask them to quote for the same number of units. As with the previous example, they may quote one for $95 and the other for $97. You may now divide the purchases among suppliers A and B (e.g., 5,000 units from A at $100 and 5,000 units from B at $95). This results in an overall saving of $2.50 per unit or an overall saving of 2.5% even without changing or squeezing Supplier A.

Currency fluctuation: Assuming that you can purchase product X from Supplier A, which is located in the USA, and from Supplier B which is located in Canada, you should keep an eye on the dollar exchange and select your supplier based on the value of the dollar. Thus, when the Canadian dollar is strong, buy from the U.S. supplier, but when the Canadian dollar is weak buy from the Canadian supplier. A dollar exchange rate as low as 3% or 5% can add a few points to your margin.

Tracking components costs: Let's assume that in some situations you can purchase product X, which is manufactured by Supplier Z. Let's further assume that product X contains one ingredient at 30%, another ingredient at 20%, and a third ingredient at 10%, for total ingredients of 60%. These ingredients may be commodities such as oil, plastic, corn, soya and chemicals. If you now track the cost of these three ingredients by month or quarter, you can determine if your supplier has lower or higher costs. Tracking ingredient costs can be done by accessing specialized databases. If you track these three ingredients over time and find that the 60% is now 55%, you can approach Supplier Z with your research and offer to share the savings of the 5% between the two of you.

Understanding price components: Reviewing the cost components of the product or service with your supplier can also lead to savings on both sides. An example of these cost components might be costs for transportation, warehousing, service or packaging. The point here is that you should sit down with your supplier and analyze the cost components of what you are purchasing together in order to identify potential areas for savings that can be split between the two of you. This is one way to find a win-win situation with suppliers.

CHAPTER 12

KPI (KEY PERFORMANCE INDICATORS)

Monitoring Your Progress

"Direction, not intention determines your destination."
— Andy Stanley

KPI (key performance indicators) is an effective tool to manage growth and navigate your business as you take it to the next level. Periods of change and transition in any arena of life tend to be filled with tension, uncertainty and doubt. The same applies to the life of the organization and our roles in it.

As a business grows, managers find themselves overwhelmed with day-to-day activities and tasks. They are constantly pushed into new territory and forced into areas that may be outside their comfort zone or expertise. They are required to take more risks and test new methods, processes and formulas in order to increase performance and productivity.

Management has to make increasingly more decisions about important issues, and do so at a fast pace with great consequences, and often with limited information at hand. This is where things have the potential to cause problems and can produce serious repercussions.

Making the wrong decisions or procrastinating about making them at all is just as damaging. Another common error is being distracted by the day-to-day on account of the overall direction of the business, along with concentrating on tactical decisions and neglecting strategic ones. These are practical examples of the many pitfalls of managing growing businesses.

Handling growth and managing it effectively is a challenge. But not knowing how to manage growth and adjust your business in order to reach the next level can be both daunting and fatal. KPI is a useful tool that can be utilized to effectively maneuver your business and better manage growth.

What is the KPI?

Every organization needs a process that monitors business performance. KPI consists of a monthly report that shows the key drivers of the business. The information is discussed by the senior management team in a monthly meeting, usually around the 7th, 8th or 9th of the month.

The KPI distills pertinent information into an accurate and concise one-page document. That document should be available before the 6th working day of the next month. It highlights all key areas that affect business performance. It also acts as a set of business gauges that is similar to a car dashboard (speed, fuel level, oil pressure, safety features).

The KPI contains the key indicators of your business, and consists of both financial and non-financial figures. It is an X-ray of your business for a given month and a given period.

Most business operators rely on the financial numbers to monitor their business performance. They concentrate primarily on the profit and loss (P&L) monthly statement. This is a good practice, but is not sufficient. Relying solely on the financial numbers leaves you with three significant shortcomings:

1) They don't provide all the necessary tools to manage the business since they only cover the financial aspect. They don't reflect customers, product line, productivity or quality. They just tell part of the story, so you are only getting some of the indicators you need to keep the company working at optimum capacity. In other words, financial numbers tell you the outcome, but not the **"why"** behind the numbers. You need to know the **"whys"** so you zero in on opportunities and challenges.

2) They are put together by financial personnel primarily for financial reasons. But management needs an overall business monitoring tool, not only a financial monitoring tool.

3) The financial numbers may only be available by the middle of the next month. In many organizations they are only available near the end of the next month. This makes the information outdated for managers who need to use it in a practical and timely way. The sooner the leadership of an organization knows the business is heading in the wrong direction, the sooner they can make changes to get back on track.

Contents of the KPI

The KPI contains financial information about revenues, gross profit, gross margin and selected key costs like manufacturing, distribution, sales, administration, overhead and operating profit. In addition, it contains selected information about inventory levels and accounts receivable.

You will also find commercial information about sales, product/service performance, sales mix, repeat business, new orders and other selective data. Finally, the KPI has key information about production, operations and overhead information as it is appropriate to the business. These items may include manufacturing costs, distribution costs, productivity levels, quality data, back orders, fill rate, work-in-progress and the number of employees.

Forecast information regarding future performance will include the revenue/sales forecast for the next 90–120 days, and other information like projects underway and work-in-progress. This section predicts future performance. The forecast will usually guide short-term decisions that influence employment levels, purchasing decisions and pricing.

The KPI could also include a segment that groups together pertinent pieces of information. This could act as an important indicator for a particular company or activity.

The KPI should highlight revenues and sales for the month and year-to-date (YTD). It should compare them to the same figures from the same month last year, and to YTD last year, your monthly target, and YTD target. The revenues would also include the sales mix, such as the main product, service lines or categories (up to a maximum of five categories). In some businesses, the geographical mix of the business is shown or the channels through which sales are generated.

It's not necessary to include all the details in the KPI. The KPI should only include key pieces of information. Ratios pertinent to the particular business should also be included, since they highlight opportunities or problems. Since this is a significant point, let's explore it further.

Let's assume you have four product lines, which in turn, are divided into 14 categories and 24 subcategories. The KPI should tell you how the month's sales performed vs. your target, and vs. the same month last year. Are we up, flat or down? Then you want to know how the four main product lines are behaving. Where do we stand vs. our yearly target and how are we doing this year vs. last year?

Some top-line analysis by volume and price can also tell you how prices are holding and how volumes are performing. This is the KPI and how it works for you. If you want to go beyond this into more detail (e.g., details on the 14 categories and 24 subcategories in our example), you should hold a sales meeting to analyze sales performance in greater detail. The KPI allows you to quickly appraise the key indicators of the entire business once a month. This means you're not only looking at financials and not only at one or two areas of the business.

What you need to know

A sample KPI can be found in the appendix.

The KPI requires customization and its sections need to be adapted to your particular business situation.

Quite often, over 70% of the contents can be the same or similar across a diverse set of organizations, but the other 30% is very important; it can determine if the KPI is a valid tool or not. It also requires some expertise to handle objections and any resistance by the managers involved.

The KPI is a useful tool, but there are situations where it is not used effectively, if at all. KPI failure is due more to lack of desire in implementing it, or to a resistant style of management.

Some presidents and general managers don't want to share confidential information with their team, and prefer not to give clear areas of accountability to their managers. This is common in private companies where ownership (usually family-owned) does not want to share detailed financial information with the management team.

Watch for potential resistance

Here in a nutshell are some common areas of resistance to implementing the KPI process. The **financial manager** by definition wants to have financial numbers with high integrity and accuracy. This is good, but they can do that only around mid-month or later in the month when they close all the books and reconcile all entries. The KPI cannot wait to be ready until the 20th or month-end.

The solution is to favor speed and settle for 95% accuracy over 100% accuracy, but with quick access to a KPI. Managers will always trade the 5% accuracy for faster delivery of the KPI. But financial managers tend to resist this trade-off. However, once they understand the benefits of having a KPI as early as possible in the month, they will cooperate.

The **sales manager** may also resist making forecasts at first. Forecasts push them outside their comfort zone and require them to involve all their team members and to predict the future. Nobody wants to forecast the future because they don't want to look foolish if they are wrong.

It is difficult to forecast, but this difficulty must be addressed as a challenge rather than an insurmountable obstacle. Practice makes perfect, and though it's not easy, it is still doable and gets easier the more you forecast. I suggest aiming for over 90% accuracy for the forecast of the current month, over 85% for one month out, over 80% for two months out and over 75% for three months out.

These margins of deviation (10%–25%) are significant. The bottom line is that a well-run business can reasonably forecast its revenues. This has nothing to do with the size of the business or the activity, but everything to do with the quality of the management and the forecasting process. Rather than getting fixed on accuracy percentage, try to get better at forecasting with time. The numbers I have given you are just examples; pinpoint your own objectives and standards and become better at forecasting your business. It will result in improved business performance.

Finally, the **president or general manager** can also resist if they don't want to share certain information with their team. The KPI is an open book with sensitive data. While there are ways to conceal some financial details, the KPI acts as a very good X-ray of the business.

One monthly meeting with all senior managers

Equally important is the fact that the KPI also involves chairing a meeting once a month with all senior managers. The meeting will usually be at least two hours and may go to three in certain situations. Some CEOs are not comfortable with this role. In such a case, the CEO needs coaching on how to effectively steer a productive KPI meeting.

When chairing this meeting, focus on the content of the KPI and stay with the overall direction of the business. Discuss if you are on track or off track, and why this is the case. Give priority and focus on the direction of the business. Focus first on getting the right direction; your speed can be worked upon once you have the direction set.

The KPI meeting should determine if the company is heading in the right direction and if we will achieve our yearly objectives. The KPI meeting is about a monthly review of the entire company, not one area. You want to review key indicators for sales, marketing, operations, finance, HR, IT and so on. This will result in a review of the whole company direction on a monthly basis.

Benefits of the KPI

Once implemented successfully, the KPI provides many benefits. It promotes greater accountability since every manager sees their area of responsibility exposed and represented by factual data. It can be very powerful when hard, comparable, indicative numbers are gathered and reported in a systematic and consistent manner.

More importantly, a manager will know the numbers pertaining to their area of responsibility, as well as the numbers from other areas of the company and from the organization as a whole. Thus, it will be obvious to everyone who is a high performer and who is not. This can be a very strong motivator and, when used correctly, a great tool for team building.

The KPI forces the management team to look at the big picture without sacrificing details. All managers are working from the same set of numbers, and working with a focus on the key issues, areas and drivers of the business. Peripheral and secondary issues fall by the wayside. No doubt they will get handled, but the team is now working with a focus and an order of priority.

The KPI also forces management to evaluate and discuss strategies, not only tactical issues. This means managers will look at results rather than only engage in activities. They can see the consequences of their decisions and how those decisions influence the business. Just as important, they can also see the effect of procrastination when decisions are not made when they should be made. Pricing actions, hiring decisions, quality measures, new product launches, margin-improvement initiatives and cost-management actions are revealed by the numbers and are now available to all team members through the KPI.

Finally, the improved ability of the business to forecast performance allows it to plan better and cultivate areas of opportunity while addressing areas of weakness. The management team then becomes more proactive, not reactive. The KPI addresses balance sheet issues and capital requirements that are needed to finance expansion.

While it's true that businesses face difficulties if they lack growth, it's also true that businesses run into trouble because they simply do not know how to manage growth.

A turnaround becomes more difficult with a heavy load of problems that are not addressed. The KPI prevents this by dealing with problems as they arise, and by helping management take preventative measures.

A one-page KPI?

I prefer the KPI to be a one-page monthly report, but sometimes the size of the company and/or complexity of the business don't allow all the key performance indicators to fit on one page. In this case, go with a two-page report. In some instances, and I say this reluctantly, three pages may be required. I want to emphasize the need to keep the KPI as a tool that is focused on the big picture. Don't put meticulous details into this report. You can have secondary tools and reports to monitor details, but that is not the purpose of the KPI.

The KPI is an excellent tool to monitor business performance and rally the management team so it will focus on the key drivers of the business. Growing the top and bottom line in a healthy manner, while strengthening the strategic position of the business, makes a successful business.

CHAPTER 13

TRAINING REVISITED

"Anyone who stops learning is old,
whether at 20 or 80. Anyone who keeps
learning stays young. The greatest thing
in life is to keep your mind young."
— Henry Ford

A few years ago, I was having lunch with a senior human resources executive who said that the company's training budget had been cut since they were experiencing revenue shortfall and lower levels of business. This is not unusual. Often the training budget is the first to go.

I couldn't help but think how wrong this was. Cutting and/or eliminating the training budget in an organization that is experiencing a shortage of revenue is like putting less gas in your car to save money. How far can you go with little gas in your tank? Not far. This same principle applies to a lack of training.

Training is the acquisition of knowledge, skills and competencies. The goal of training is to improve one's capabilities, capacity and performance.

Training should be one of the first investments made to maintain company success or bring an organization back into the black. In a crisis situation, cutting expenses is absolutely necessary, but leadership should think twice about cutting training costs. Instead, allocate more funds to training teams. While this may seem counterintuitive, you will find that even in hard times such a training strategy works every time.

I will discuss some of the main reasons for going against the grain — not slashing the training budget but investing in training is a desirable course of action.

The first rule in solving problems is to get to the real heart of the problem or obstacle. It's obvious that if revenues are soft, expenses must be reduced. But the key is to determine what expenses to cut. Training provides the muscle you need to keep a top-performing pace.

If the real issue is that revenues are not growing or are declining, then that is the problem you should focus on and fix. Don't blame it on the training budget. Maybe the quality of your products and services has deteriorated or perhaps a competitor is offering better value. The bottom line is that you have to get to the root of what causes softness of sales. Cutting or reducing the training budget is a temporary fix that will only contribute further to the decline of revenues down the road.

In any business, one of the key objectives is to outdo your competitors by offering better value. Competitors can easily copy your winning recipe by acquiring similar machinery, offering free delivery, opening nearby stores or copying your advertising message. They can duplicate your tangible and physical assets and promotions. However, what they cannot replicate is your unique blend and brand of people skills, experience and motivation. They can hire qualified people, but they can't duplicate your team.

This is where to develop a competitive edge. Your people are what make the difference.

No sports team would cut or reduce training. It is in training where you prepare the team to win a game. No coach in his right mind would say, "We need to cut expenses, so let's skip our practice." In the same vein, I am not sure why an executive might think that cutting or reducing training expenses would be profitable. An ongoing investment in training will prove to be a positive move for the organization.

Although some accountants would not agree with me, I believe **training is an investment rather than an operating cost**. Investment in training should be capitalized and carried on the balance sheet and amortized over several years just like fixed assets (e.g., machinery, equipment, vehicles, computers, etc.). Maybe not all training costs can be treated as investments, but many training investments will result in increased value for several years. That is why they should be carried as a fixed asset.

Let's review the different types of training:

- **Induction and orientation training:** This is training for new employees to introduce them to the company, its products, policies, systems and the organization in general.
- **Job training:** This is training for new employees in a specific position in order to train them on job tasks and responsibilities required for the role. The training gives them the knowledge and skills needed to do their job effectively.
- **Safety training:** This is training for employees that will minimize accidents and promote a safe environment. It includes fire and disaster drills.
- **Promotional training:** This is training for newly promoted employees to teach them the skills of the new job.
- **Refresher training:** This is training or a refresher course that will update employees on new technologies, systems and methods that contribute to improved productivity and/or quality.
- **Remedial training:** This is training for employees that will overcome shortcomings in behavior or improve sub-par performance.
- **Internship:** This is training for new or experienced employees that involves completing a specific program to keep them up to date on developments within their job requirements.

These different types of training highlight the importance of each one and also highlight their role in keeping the organization fit so it will serve customers profitably and with excellence. Cutting the appropriate training method will simply weaken the team and reduce the effectiveness of the organization. The fact that the lack of training is not immediately visible is no reason to delay or reduce it.

In all organizations the performance of people is in direct relationship to customer satisfaction. Factory workers may not have direct contact with customers, but their output influences the satisfaction of their customers, while frontline employees have a more direct impact on customer satisfaction. However, both determine how profitable the company will be and how satisfied the customers will be.

Anyone coming into a company for the first time can quickly tell if a business has invested in training employees or instead has cut corners on training.

Here are some examples of poor training:

- You call a company and the receptionist mumbles her name. She asks with an annoyed and unpleasant voice if she can help you. Thirty minutes of simple training on telephone manners would change this situation from a negative to a positive.
- You are looking for a sales associate in a big retail store and when an employee sees you, they run to hide or change aisles in order to avoid you. Employees should not run away from customers, but should run to serve them. Steve Jobs once said, "Get closer than ever to your customers. So close, in fact, that you tell them what they need well before they realize it themselves."
- You bring an item to the cash register and wait until the two employees standing there finish their conversation before they are ready to serve you. You feel like you have interrupted their discussion and should apologize for the inconvenience. Training should include what Henry Ford once said: "It is not the employer who pays the wages. Employers only handle the money. It is the customer who pays the wages." This is Training 101!
- You call a 1-800 Customer Care number and discover that you have to go through a maze of instructions just to get help. Navigating through complicated automated systems is harrowing enough. But what's worse is when you must wade through various telephone prompts and then wait an incredibly long time before speaking with a live person. Then you find that the person does not have the skill or knowledge to help you. They say you didn't get the right number and must start the automated process again with a new number because they can't transfer you. Or they simply don't know how to help you. Customer service departments should be a hub of continuous training with product and technological knowledge updated regularly. Such departments should be equipped to handle difficult clients and do problem solving.

- In some big companies, the customer service call center is designed to direct you to their website because they don't want to talk to customers. They are missing out on a great opportunity. The more you engage with customers, the clearer things become and the easier it is to see what you should be doing. Senior managers need serious training and should vigorously apply themselves to streamlining the customer care process for consumer ease.

These are examples of an organization that has made huge cuts to their basic training budget and to developing employee skills. It's only a matter of time before this company closes its doors for good. A simple rule dictates, **If we do not take care of our customers, someone else will.**

In today's business world, technology improvements and lower communication costs make good training a more effective and affordable proposition than ever before. Review the following points:

a) **Training can be provided via the Internet** with online seminars and video conferencing from across the world. Videos can be easily downloaded on laptops and mobile devices. Employees can learn new skills remotely and update their existing knowledge and more without setting foot in a classroom.

b) Organizations can hire **professional trainers, experts and consultants** for fixed assignments on a daily or hourly basis, as needed. Many training resources come with flexible options that have proven training methods. Because of the access to technology that we have today, we can obtain all this in any language from any location worldwide.

c) You can introduce **coaching and mentoring programs** that have been developed and perfected over the years for a fraction of their original costs. This is due to a wide global distribution of training material. Programs that were only available to large organizations and corporations a few years ago are now available at very reasonable prices to small and medium-size companies. Some of it is even available for free through websites and YouTube, but first you should ensure that these methods have been tried and proven and are approved by respected people.

These new training programs, courses and seminars are not only applicable to your frontline employees, but are also available to your managers, executives, board members and the most senior positions in your organization. One-on-one **coaching** and mentoring allows you to get feedback and to acquire knowledge and insights in a customized manner. It also positions you to continue developing ongoing relationships and attitude development.

Organizations should ask this key question: **Are you tracking and measuring your organization's performance and your people's productivity?** If you can improve the sales-closing ratio of your salespeople from 1:8 to 1:4, what would that do to your revenues? Just imagine transforming every customer complaint into a new sale! With the right training of your staff, complaining customers can represent a huge opportunity for more business.

Regular and solid training programs are one way that an organization can build itself from within by treating employees with respect and dignity. Employees who feel empowered, equipped and valued are happy employees.

This happiness is reflected in the customer service that takes place both inside and outside the organization. Colleagues and coworkers will quickly and efficiently help each other, and deliver on promises to each other. This also results in positive energy extended to those outside the organization.

If customers are happy, there is a greater chance of increased profitability, and this only leads to satisfied shareholders. This chain reaction will set an organization up so it has the ability to make good investments that sustain the company's success. Indeed, training is the catalyst for sustaining an organization's long-term success.

CHAPTER 14

CHOOSING YOUR BANKER, ACCOUNTANT, LAWYER AND CONSULTANTS

"Follow your heart but take your brain with you."
— Anonymous

This chapter is about managing the relationship with your banker, lawyer, accountant and any advisors or consultants you may use. External advisors can provide excellent assistance and expertise and help you achieve your corporate and personal objectives.

It is wise to surround yourself with well-qualified, experienced, trustworthy advisors who bring excellent added value to your team. These advisors and experts, in their own areas of specialization, will be more effective if you (a) develop a strong and healthy relationship with them, and (b) keep them updated on your corporate progress and future plans.

Selecting the right person

The best way to recruit and build this team of advisors is to get to know them when you don't need them. If you wait until you do, you will be influenced by an immediate need and the subject that requires their expertise. Recruiting an advisor at the last minute is counterproductive because the issue you seek advice for will take priority. I recommend you meet these advisors as early as possible so as to select them before your need. An exploratory meeting is often all it takes to find out if the advisor has the qualifications you need, and if there is chemistry between the two of you.

Selecting legal counsel

Good lawyers come with different expertise — one size does not fit all. Lawyers have specializations including litigation, patents, corporate, international, immigration, contracts and taxation, to name a few. Just as with a sports team, some lawyers are excellent at attacking while others are better at defending. For example, if you plan to make acquisitions over the next five years, you need a good corporate lawyer with successful acquisition/divestiture experience under their belt. Your litigation lawyer may be excellent, but acquisition work is different than litigation, so you need the right expertise.

You need to choose your senior team players well in advance of the game. Selecting the players at the last moment or without doing your homework is very risky and can actually be damaging.

The French connection

When I was heading a business unit in France, I asked if we had considered making acquisitions in order to gain market share and consolidate our market position. Senior executives in the head office told me, "Acquisitions do not work in France! The French are very protective of their companies and our past attempts failed." I couldn't believe that, so I asked my senior team in France the same question. They provided a much different reason why previous attempts to make acquisitions had failed.

They said the acquisition lawyers were a law firm from Texas, and that the Texan contingent that visited France wore hats and boots and smoked cigars, and needed translators since none of them spoke French. The people leading the acquisition discussion were flown in from the U.S. and were, to say the least, out of tune with local French market conditions. We decided to change our strategy and tactics by giving our first project in target acquisition to a French senior executive on my team. We also hired a French law firm. In addition, we gathered references from some long-term French clients including the French ministry of foreign affairs, the ministry of interior and the central bank of France. In less than 120 days we successfully made our first French acquisition — *et voilà*!

The choice of advisors is key to your success, especially on dossiers where the outcome is strategic and you don't get a second chance. Over my long career, I often changed my advisors depending on the nature of the mission or battlefield conditions. Without a doubt, the choice of advisors was vital to our success.

An informal breakfast or lunch meeting

It all starts with an informal meeting to get to know each other, and to know the capabilities of our respective companies. You can usually find an intermediary who can introduce you to the right person. An informal breakfast or lunch is the best way to evaluate the potential advisor in a reserved and elegant manner.

During the meeting you can volunteer information about yourself and provide a brief overview of your company. Once your guest is at ease, you can ask about their career, experience and for an overview of their firm, its services, their clients, and their wins. Advisors are keen to talk and will voluntarily share information if you are a good listener.

Don't make the breakfast or lunch sound like an interrogation, but make sure the information flows both ways. Once the meeting is over, write all the key information you have assembled while it is still fresh in your mind. Don't trust your memory; write down the information you gathered along with the impression you got from the discussion. If you are planning to interview other advisors, ask the same questions so you can compare the answers before selecting the right advisor.

In that first meeting, avoid asking about prices and fees. Instead, keep the focus on qualitative information such as experience, examples of projects handled, examples of challenges and solutions, capabilities, resources and any other important factors you can think of. There will be ample time to discuss prices and fees later. Do not hire cheap, but aim to recruit the best.

You may also reflect on the size of the law firm. If you select a very large firm, they may be able to offer a wide array of specializations under one roof but will also have big fees to match and may treat you as a small client. On the other hand, a small firm may render a more personalized service with lower fees, but may not have all the specializations you need. I prefer using mid-size firms that can offer a good range of specializations and provide a good service while offering reasonable rates.

What about the bank?

Choosing both your bank and your main contact at that bank is an important decision. Not all banks are the same, and please don't select your bank only on the basis of their interest rate. While all banks will adhere to the same legislation and have more or less the same values and fundamental principles of lending, they still differ.

Some banks are friendlier than others, some are more risk tolerant than others, and they all have different corporate cultures in the same way that legal firms have their specializations, along with their strong and weak points.

For instance, some banks are mainly domestic ones while others are international. If your banking needs are mainly domestic, a national bank will probably fit your needs. But if you'll be doing a lot of export/import or international and global business, you need a bank with international experience, global reach and worldwide branches. Some banks are also specialized by business sector.

For example, some banks specialize in the old economy (i.e., agriculture, mining, food, manufacturing and farming sectors) and understand the ins and outs of these sectors. Others may be specialized in the new economy in such fields as high tech, the service industry, technology and communication.

In selecting your bank, it is best to work with two banks rather than one so you are less vulnerable to sudden changes in your bank's vision, mission and strategic direction.

While we are on this subject, give some thought to the type of loan you need in order to make the right choices on the type of financing (demand loans, term loans, long-term loans, etc.). Your bank may advise you about a certain type of a loan, but that may be influenced by their needs rather than yours.

Thus, it is important to select the right type of financing and make the decision with your accountant/auditor who can also advise you on the best type of financing according to your present and future needs. I have often seen many of my clients make decisions and select financing options that are based primarily on interest rates and/or short-term objectives. It would be more beneficial for them to evaluate all the factors involved in taking on debt, and then address the short, medium and long-term needs of their company.

This is especially true and important when you deal with venture capital firms that want to realize very high rates of return in excess of 45% or 50% in order to fundamentally compensate for the many investments that go bad!

What I suggested earlier for selecting and building a relationship with your legal counsel also applies to your banker. Keep your bank up to date on your progress and build a relationship with the people at the bank. This is very important.

Meeting with your banker at least twice a year is also a must.

Bank loans

Generally, bank loans come in two different kinds: demand loans and term loans.

A demand loan is usually secured by your accounts/receivable and inventory and is mainly used to supplement your working capital. Demand loans, as the name may indicate, can be recalled by the bank at any time. When this happens you will have to scramble to pay them, whether you have the money or not. That means you must find somebody else to lend you the money to repay the original bank. While banks don't recall their loans without reason, they can, so be careful when obtaining a demand loan. A demand loan is often in the form of a line of credit that allows you to borrow a little more depending on your need, as long as you don't exceed your limit.

A term loan is a loan with a fixed repayment schedule for a fixed period of time (e.g., three years, five years, seven years or more). It is similar to your home mortgage. For example, you borrow $50,000 repayable over a five-year period (i.e., repaying $10,000 per year in principle plus interest). As long as you pay the monthly interest and principle, the bank cannot recall the loan. Fixed-term loans are usually used to purchase fixed assets such as machinery, equipment, building, land, etc., and are usually secured by hard assets like — you guessed it — machinery, equipment, building, land, etc. A fixed-term loan can also be obtained to finance a specific strategy, succession plan, expansion or acquisition. Unlike the line of credit loan, the fixed-term loan is dispensed 100% and then repaid back according to the repayment schedule. **It does not allow for drawings to go up or down based on your needs like a line of credit loan.**

What do banks look for?

When banks lend money — whether demand loans or term loans — there are two fundamental things that concern them:

1) Your ability to pay the loan and interest back, and 2) the degree of risk they are taking by extending you the loan (i.e., what is the security if things do not go right?). They want to know if the loan is secured by enough assets. And in cases where you default on your repayment, what security do they have? Keep these two elements in mind.

Let's say that a bank extends a line of credit (demand loan) for $200K when your accounts receivables (A/R) and inventory are $150K and $180K respectively. This means that the bank has security of $330K for the line of credit of $200K ($150K + $180K = $330K). How is this? It is because the bank is willing to finance only 80% of your A/R (80% of $150K = $120K) and 50% of your inventory (50% of $180K = $90K), which makes both securities worth a total of $210,000.

Banks have their own internal ratios for calculating their measure for security. But on many occasions, as in our example, the bank security was fine when the A/R was $150K and inventory $180K. But with time and growth these two assets grew to $250K and $250K respectively. So, would the line of credit be increased accordingly? It should, but in many cases the line of credit increases but not at the same proportion as the increase in receivables and inventory. This gives the bank a greater margin of security but short-changes you the client.

I don't say this to make you upset with your bank, but to explain that you can manage the relationship as a win-win for both sides. A bank will not volunteer this type of information. It is up to you to do your homework and evaluate the details of the financing, and the needed security to be pledged. Security must be reasonable. What is reasonable will vary according to your credit rating, years in business, your business performance and so on. This is why I suggest having two banks, so you have better options and alternatives at your disposal. You also have two friends instead of one!

For a term loan, the bank will usually want you to advance a portion of the purchase price of the asset, with the bank financing the rest.

For example, you purchase a building worth $500,000 by investing $100,000 of your money (20% of the value of the asset) and getting a mortgage of $400,000 from the bank (80% of the value of the assets. In this situation, the bank takes a security that is 20% higher than the market value. As time goes by, you pay back the loan, your debt decreases and usually the value of the real estate and building will appreciate, giving the bank a higher security than required. In our example, after five years the mortgage debt may be down to $300,000 while the market value of the building may have grown to $600,000. This means the bank is holding a security of $600,000 for a loan of $300,000. That's fine, but you should know that you have a larger equity and also that this asset has room to obtain new financing and more borrowing capability. If you need capital, there is room to refinance.

You can look at banks and financing companies as companies that are in the business of "selling money." No more, no less. Bankers may not like the way I put it, but fundamentally that is what they sell. Money!

Bank fees

Banks makes their money in two ways. First, they collect or buy money for let's say 2%, and then turn around and sell it for 5%, which makes in this example a 60% margin (buy at $2 and sell at $5, making $3 gross profit or 60% gross margin). Second, by charging their customers fees to pay for the cost of services they provide.

I recommend going with the suggested fees at first. Don't start the relationship with arguments. It's better to go with the flow. These fees will not make you rich or poor. Once you have grown your business and proven that you are an excellent client, then negotiate for better fees and compare that to what other banks are willing to offer. All banks are "experts" at charging fees and also for inventing fees for everything under the sun. That's fine, but do your homework and compare. In other words, aim before you shoot!

Selecting your accountants and auditors

This is another key decision that can make a big difference. Just as we considered the size of the firm for legal counsel, consider the size of the accounting firm. If your company is not one of the Fortune 500, a mid-size firm is usually the better choice. An accounting firm that is too small may mean they can't serve you as you grow and require more expert services. However, a large accounting firm may not render the personalized service you need.

Most importantly, in choosing the right accounting firm, check their reputation and the type of clients they serve. An accounting firm with a good reputation with the tax department (CRA in Canada and IRS in the U.S.) is a blessing, while an accounting firm with a poor history with the tax department may wind up with the taxman auditing you.

I will never forget a consulting assignment a few years ago for an international client. I was reviewing a potential investment for my client and doing due diligence on their potential future partners. My research showed that the investment was attractive and had good partners and overall limited risk. Everything looked good. But when I arranged for a meeting with the accountant and legal counsel, we discovered that my client had received poor advice in the past from his original accountant. Proceeding with the suggested investment would have put him in a risky and unfavorable condition with the taxman. My client had to pass on the investment opportunity in order to correct his own situation before making future investments.

Why did this happen? It happened because my client hired a small accounting firm that was cutting corners and offering bad advice. Good, sound advice, even if a little expensive, is key to your success. Bad advice at a low price isn't worth it. Bad advice can put you in the wrong direction, which will cost you more money when you make a U-turn.

You should meet with your accountant at least twice a year. Update the accountant on your past achievements and share your future plans. Some accountants are historical accountants, meaning that they are good with past and present procedures, while others are known to be future accountants. Future accountants are helpful because they are more strategic thinkers and can advise you on the best way to position yourself for future plans. In any business, you need both types. You need the discipline and steadiness of the first type, and the skills and ability to see the future of the second type. If your accountant can provide both, that's a gem!

Your accountant can advise on how to set your accounting system to prepare your year-end financials and how to be set up in a way to help you analyze revenues and costs intelligently. The accountant can also advise on these things: your corporate structure that will give you additional flexibility when growing the business or divesting part of it, your fiscal policy to reduce your tax burden, your exposure to currency fluctuation, your insurance needs, your banking relationship, and many more important subjects.

Keep your accountant up to date on your performance and your strategic plan, and ask them to contribute to your success by suggesting and recommending actions that will help you achieve your objectives.

A good rule is to select your lawyer, accountant and banker with the same spirit you use in selecting your doctor. You would not choose a doctor without doing some due diligence and you would certainly not choose them for their low fees.

Surround yourself and your business with external counselors, consultants and advisors who are experienced, trustworthy and committed to your success. This will multiply your resources and let you have access to sound resources. Having a strong team of external advisors is like a turbo engine. When you drive normally, the turbo is not utilized, but when you need the power and the extra power it is there on demand.

What about consultants?

The key to your success is to select consultants, mentors and business coaches who provide specific expertise, help you develop your skills and contribute to the professional growth of key members of your team. Choose people who are not only experienced, but who are successful in consulting with a solid track record and impeccable ethics.

Of course, there are no perfect consultants. But what differentiates one consultant from another is the presence of all three key requirements: experience, a proven track record and adherence to high ethical and professional standards.

In selecting a coach or mentor, pick one who listens, questions and challenges. Make sure they will help you become a better manager or executive. And pick someone who will push you outside your comfort zone. A coach should not be afraid to ask questions and share observations.

I also recommend that a written report be produced after each coaching session, so you have a paper trail and record of key subjects discussed and important recommendations that were made. Written notes help make us more accountable for what we promised to do or to not continue. The written notes don't need to be long or extensive. But they should be accurate, up to date and informative. They can be in bullet form and one or two pages long, which should be more than enough per session.

Remember that one of the secrets of succeeding in a coaching assignment is that you must be coachable. In other words, be willing to look at yourself and discuss your strengths, weaknesses, fears, habits and passions.

You must also be committed to dedicating the right amount of time to your coaching sessions. Coaching is an investment you make willingly and with enthusiasm. External advisors and experts are an excellent resource. They can be an extension to your senior team and can be on demand since they are not on the payroll. They are a variable cost, which is better defined as a good investment.

Keep in mind that you don't have to implement their advice or recommendations — you can still decide to differ with them. The important benefit, however, is that you now have more knowledge and a different perspective and method. Whatever your decision is, it will be a better one.

CHAPTER 15

ONLINE PRESENCE

Your Website: A Key Marketing Tool

"If your business is not on the Internet,
then your business will be out of business."
— Bill Gates

A few years back people would open the Yellow Pages to find a restaurant, a doctor, an attorney or a bakery. Today they go to a search engine like Google to find products and services they need. Once they find what they want, they open any business' website to get more information: prices, menus, special offers, contact information, and services.

They don't even need to have a PC. They can do all this from the convenience of their smartphone in real time. They look at reviews by other customers and read what other people say about the business. I have often changed my mind about a restaurant based on feedback readily available on the Internet.

Research indicates that 90% of business-to-business (B2B) purchase decisions start with a search engine and that 80% of people search local business online.

All businesses need a professional website with a "wow"

With this in mind, there is no doubt that all businesses should have a website and not just any website, but a professional one that can attract new and repeat customers. No website would be like a business with no sign on its door. Besides, why would you not have a website that is open 24/7 and that can keep prospects, customers, suppliers, employees and all your business associates up to date on your company?

Remember that it's not that your business needs a website as much as your customers and prospects are expecting your company to have one.

Your website is one of the best and most efficient marketing tools available in order to "wow" your prospects and customers before they even meet or talk with you. For many businesses, customers and prospects can be located halfway around the world and they may have a genuine interest in your product or service. Your target market doesn't have to be limited by geography: It can be international. This may not apply to all businesses, but you will be surprised with how the Internet has taken companies from the local scene to the global market almost overnight.

What an opportunity

To a large extent, websites tend to level the playing field for big and small companies. How?

Well, if I visit the IBM website I can see it on the small screen of my smartphone just as I can see my own website, HughLatif.com. If I visit the McKinsey & Company website from my laptop, I can see it on the same 17-inch screen monitor that I use to see HughLatif.com! While McKinsey & Company is huge when compared to Hugh Latif & Associates, when it comes to visiting our respective websites, we are both limited by the same equipment and use fundamentally the same technology.

And Google finds both of our websites with the same speed. Consider the different sizes of these two management consulting practices. Google actually has relatively better coverage of Hugh Latif & Associates (3 pages) than of McKinsey's because McKinsey has so many competitors fighting for space and ads on the Google search result page! Unbelievable, but true. I'm not talking about search ranking, I'm talking about the number of results Hugh Latif & Associates has (at the last I checked, 473,000 vs. McKinsey's 1.2M).

Website don'ts

Watch out though, because a poorly designed website or an unattractive, non-professional website can cause more damage than good. I often visit websites and see information that hasn't been updated for years. What does this say to customers, prospects and potential employees who visit your website?

What about a website that has empty pages or poor images and photos? What about websites with information that is cramped on the page, text that is hard to see and read, no titles, and an overall sense of being user-unfriendly?

These are counterproductive websites and can cause important business to flee from you. You've heard that you don't have a second chance at making a positive impression. It is the same for a website visit. Unfortunately, you don't get a second chance, and the homepage may invite the visitor to stay longer and visit more of your website, or exit quickly. Similarly, if you walk down Main Street, some store windows are inviting and entice you to walk in while others make you walk on.

Website do's

With some of the website don'ts out of the way, here is a list of website do's. They are shown in random order and I believe all are important, so don't skip any points:

- Let's start with your **domain name**. It is better that your domain name be simple and no more than 14 letters. It should also be free of commas, dots and hyphens. Simple, easy and short is best.
- Make sure you **register your domain name** with a reputable company and have a bring-forward file to remind you of its expiry date. Website domain-name pirates can blackmail you for your own website name if the domain name expires without prior renewal.
- Make sure you **host** your website with a reputable Internet hosting company that will have your website up 99% of the time, and that your website loads quickly.

- You know your customers and prospects well, so make sure your website appeals to **your audience** in look, feel, content, graphics, etc. If your main audience is mainly middle-age professionals, use a conservative and relatively large font for easy reading. And use conservative colors. If your audience is mainly teenagers, use a funkier font with more jazzy colors. Adapt to your audience.
- Make sure your website displays well on **mobile devices** like smartphones and tablets.
- The **look and feel** of your website should be a continuation of your sales and marketing material with the same colors, logos and fonts. In this way there is harmony and continuity with your marketing material.
- Pay particular importance and care to the **content** of your website and get professional help, not only for the typos and grammar, but for the style and wording.
- Choose a **graphic designer** who understands your business and understands what you expect from your website. You are not competing for the website design of the year. Clear design, a fresh look and easy to read are best.
- Use headings to **organize** your page content and stay away from cramped information on a page. Focus on the most important information first, then add the supporting details, and finally fill it in with more useful information. Keep superfluous information out — less is more. Use the "read more" button to keep pages clear and easy to read, and when appropriate use bullet points.
- **Hyperlinked text** makes for a user-friendly website.
- Use professional **photos and videos**. No amateur photos and videos, and don't stretch professional photos. If using videos, short videos of two to three minutes maximum are best. If videos are used, they must load quickly. If loading takes more than a minute, 80% of your visitors will exit.
- Optimize performance with **search engines** by including the right search-engine words in your website content (SEO). Give search engines what they are looking for.
- Have your **company name, full address and phone number** on the footer of all pages for easy reference.
- Use **call to action buttons** when appropriate or opt-in list building forms.

- For **money matters** such as shopping carts and wish list, use ready-made solutions provided by well-known and reputable companies. No need to reinvent the wheel again unless you have a unique product that requires a customized e-commerce shopping cart, but that is often expensive and time-consuming.
- If you have a **search button**, make sure you test it with your website content and have a friendly phrase when the search is negative.
- Always have a **thank you phrase** when visitors send you a message or access some interactive content, so they know their request or message went through.
- Have your **main menu** of buttons clear and visible, preferably up on the home page, for easy access. Repeat the menu, if need be, in smaller font in the footer of the website.
- If you use a **drop-down menu**, make sure it is user friendly and works with every computer mouse and other accessories.
- If you have documents to give away, have them in **PDF** format. If your visitor prints them, they will print perfectly.
- Have the **CONTACT** button clearly shown at the top and/or at the footer of the page. Don't hide it in the corporate page. You want to make it easy for visitors to contact you. If computer-generated traffic bothers you, that's OK; that's the price you pay for good traffic.
- Have a separate page for **employment and careers**, and enable potential applicants to send you their résumé/CV.
- Make sure you include a page with a long list of **testimonials**. Prospects do read them. Make sure they are authentic testimonials and comments.
- If you offer **guarantees and/or warranties**, make sure these are clear.
- If your company is **affiliated with associations** and trade organizations, make sure you list them and have their logo or name hyperlinked for easy and friendly linkage.
- If your business is international, have a **translated version** available in the languages that are needed.
- If you have a **1-800 telephone number**, include it and show the hours of service and the zones covered. If you don't have an international 1-800 number, show a separate number for international phone inquiries. Make sure the employees who respond to the telephone call can speak the languages that cover your demo target.

- In your **corporate profile** show your values, vision and mission, if appropriate. If you have a code of ethics, publish it.
- If your business has been around for some time, show your starting date and show that you are a **well-established business**.
- Never lie about your size. Make sure all information on your website is **factual and correct**.
- If you can show **case studies** and actual examples about your product or service, include them in a summary format, and show before and after.
- If you operate your business from home, make sure you have a **mailing address**, preferably a physical address. You can use a virtual office address for a very low monthly charge. It offers a professional look.
- Don't use your personal phone. Have a business telephone number and make sure you have a **professional answering service** Monday to Friday, 9–5. It is a small monthly investment for a professional image.
- If you have a resource centre, post valuable articles and technical information. If you are covered by the media, share this and have a section that highlights important milestones.
- If a **frequently asked questions** section applies to your business, have an FAQ page with easy access and a friendly look.
- If you have **YouTube** videos or other **social media** content, provide friendly updated links.

That may be a long list, but I trust that all these points are important and practical and will help you bring your best website to fruition.

CHAPTER 16

ADVISORY BOARDS

Your Secret Weapon for Success

"Excellence is not a single act but a habit."
— Aristotle

The economic landscape of the world has undergone a lot of change during the last few years. North American and global economies are slowly coming out of the recessionary environments of circa 2008 when companies like General Motors (value at bankruptcy $90B), Chrysler (value at bankruptcy $29B), American Airlines ($24B in assets), RIM (Research in Motion lost over 70% of its market value) and Lehman Brothers ($690B in assets) went bankrupt. A few years back companies like Nortel and Swiss Air became insolvent. One must ask: How did corporations that size go bust?

Check the 15 largest corporations worldwide and you'll see that a third of them are in trouble. How? These corporations have all the elements of success such as strong brand names, access to capital, the latest technology, intellectual assets, strong markets and worldwide resources. They either possess what is needed to be successful, or have the resources to acquire any missing links that can contribute to their success. So why are they still in trouble?

The business media highlighted many reasons, such as lack of strategy, following the wrong strategies, poor execution of strategies, incompetent senior management and a rapid change in market conditions or technological takeovers. While all these are reasons for organizational ill health, it is more accurate to diagnose these reasons as symptoms rather than the cause.

More often than not, you will find at the heart of these challenged corporations a board of directors that has become too comfortable and asleep at the wheel. This is the real cause of the problems that drive companies into the ground.

So what is the primary role of a board of directors or an advisory board? The board has six specific key functions:

1) **Review** and **approve** the company (or organization) strategy.
2) **Monitor** the company's performance and **evaluate** management.
3) **Authorize** compensation.
4) **Ensure** the company complies with all laws and regulations, maintains high integrity of the financial numbers, adheres to ethical standards and ensures that risks are properly evaluated.
5) Provide **advice and counsel** to management.
6) Make appropriate **recommendations** to shareholders.

It is worth noting that the role of the board is not to create strategies, but to approve the strategies developed by senior management, and then monitor the quality of execution of these strategies by management. When we look at these six functions, we may conclude that the boards of these large companies failed to fulfill their primary role.

Here is one example of an organization's board that failed to fulfill its role.

Let us just imagine that you are a member of the board of a major auto manufacturer such as GM. How difficult would it be to ask the following questions and then formulate the corresponding strategies?

1) Our **hourly labor cost** is double the hourly labor cost of our competitors. Strategy 1: We need to implement a strategy that will **reduce our labor cost** to within +/– 5% of our competitors. Whether we are unionized or not isn't the question. We need to work with our unions to be competitive.

2) **The price of oil** may fluctuate for the short term, but it is safe to predict that it will most likely increase over the long term, hence customers' needs will continue to shift to smaller, more economical cars. Our present car line-up contains only 10% or less small cars. Strategy 2: We should **increase our small car line-up** and increase this percentage aggressively over the next three to seven years.
3) Customer preference worldwide is changing. In general, customers will be looking for different types of cars with alternative engines. Strategy 3: We should **invest in alternative engine technology** such as electric engines. We need to bring electric and hybrid products to the market faster.
4) Most, if not all, our competitors have **one or a maximum of two brand** names while we market our product line with more than eight brand names. And we have eight organizations and eight cost structures. Yet our competitors are profitable and we are not. Strategy 4: We should **simplify our marketing mix by reducing the number of brands we carry**.
5) It seems that the present **management team is convinced** that we need to produce many millions of auto units in order to become profitable, but how come smaller competitors are profitable producing a much lower number of units? Strategy 5: We **must lower our break-even point** significantly and succeed in making a profit at an appropriately reduced volume.
6) We have been **losing market share** consistently over the past 20 years. Strategy 6: We need to **change the sales and marketing strategies and tactics** we have been using and introduce new ones.
7) This will hurt! When we compare the compensation and **remuneration levels** of our senior management to the compensation and remuneration of our competitors, it is evident that our compensation is much higher. Strategy 7: **We need to review our compensation to senior management and bring it in line with key competitors.**

Now GM may be in need of even more strategic initiatives, but these seven easy observations and straightforward strategies could have made a big difference.

The many clients I have served were in diversified lines of businesses, and most of my consulting assignments consisted of helping companies formulate strategies to fuel sales and profit growth. Once these assignments were completed successfully and the clients' businesses had returned to growth in sales and profits, the challenge was to sustain good performance. Just like in a soccer game, it is one thing to score a goal, but another thing to defend your winning position until a final victory is secured.

You need to keep your strategy and tactics updated because nothing is constant in business except change.

Your competition will most likely regroup and be back to attack. And over time customers will be more demanding as more options become available in the marketplace. Rapid improvements in technology may help competitors, and a new crop of ideas is always springing up.

In today's global marketplace, size is not a guarantee for success. If large corporations with access to many resources miss the mark, how can privately owned, medium-sized businesses sustain good performance with fewer resources?

Creating an advisory board that provides professional counsel to management and to whom management is accountable, will provide a definite competitive edge in staying nimble and sharp.

Global marketplace

While the global economy represents an immense threat to medium-sized businesses, it also offers incredible opportunities. One example is the ease with which companies can use technology, telecommunication, transportation and free trade to compete on a worldwide basis in order to leapfrog over major competition.

On the one hand, you are no longer competing with domestic or regional competitors, but competing with companies halfway around the world. These are global companies that you did not even know existed.

Technology

When a potential client accesses a website, whether it is your small or mid-sized company, or the website of a global powerhouse like IBM, they view it on the same computer monitor, smartphone screen or tablet. In effect, IBM has the same space as you to pitch their resources and capabilities. Such technology has been a great equalizing force, and now companies of any size have access to a level playing field, which creates undeniable opportunities.

Speed

Speed of execution is another significant area that requires thorough examination. It took a company like Salesforce.com less than ten years to reach sales of $1B, and it principally sells a business service through the Internet. Google today is trading at +/– $500 a share, while Microsoft is trading around $30 a share. These examples clearly demonstrate that the rules for succeeding in today's global and dynamic marketplace have changed.

An advisory board brings a decisive competitive advantage to a privately owned and privately managed mid-size company.

Here are seven skills or key functions that a well-balanced advisory board can provide to the owners and managers of mid-size, privately owned companies:

1) **Financial:** It is not enough to have orderly accounting books in order to compete in today's aggressive marketplace. Senior financial wisdom, adequate financing, intelligent budgets, in-depth cost analysis and flexible and sharp procurement processes are also required. Just having experience is not enough. Organizations need both experience and up-to-date financial knowledge. You may not be able to afford a full-time senior CFO, but you can retain a senior and experienced CFO for ten days a year in the form of a member of your advisory board.
2) **Sales and marketing:** In a world where your competitor is thousands of miles across the globe, you require well-honed, competitive intelligence to find out what they are currently doing and what they most likely are going to do in the future. It's like a game of chess. You have

to anticipate your opponent's next move. Social media marketing has revolutionized the basic fundamentals of marketing and advertising. You need to constantly update your sales and marketing strategies. Here again, you may not be able to afford a senior sales executive or the full service of a marketing, advertising and communication firm, but you can retain a senior marketing executive for a few working days a year. Once familiar with your company, your vision for the company and your strategic plan, they can advise you at a senior level in a way that can help you avoid the pitfalls of expansion. They can suggest sales and marketing strategies, as well as tactics that are proven to be effective.

3) **Operations management:** In a global marketplace, it is not sufficient to achieve a productivity gain of two or three points a year to stay ahead. You need to aggressively reinvent yourself by investing in up-to-date technology and training and developing your team with fresh strategies. Take the reinvention further. Make sure you achieve results with optimum safety and adherence to increasing regulations while also being as "green" as possible. Expert help can make a difference to your cost structure and assist your productivity and product quality. A consultant in the area of lean manufacturing can be retained part-time or consulted a few days a year.
4) **Technology:** Technology is moving at an incredible pace. How can your local IT person possibly stay up to date when technology changes overnight? Making use of the latest technology in a practical and efficient manner can be a smart move. New technologies can help you save money or do a better job with less. For example, take the ability to teleconference with GoToMeetings.com or Skype or Google Hangout, instead of traveling to meet face-to-face. Or the instant translation website that can translate documents with 80% accuracy in a few seconds. That means leaving only 20% of a document requiring editing. There are also videos that can be easily produced and made available via YouTube for training purposes, customer service or short advertising. How about using a number of powerful IT systems now available on the cloud for a fraction of the costs from a few years back? An experienced senior IT professional on your advisory board can keep you and your IT manager up to date for a real competitive edge with technology.

5) **Human Resources Management:** Having the right people in key places has always been at the heart of any successful business. In various sectors of the marketplace, skilled labor and knowledgeable workers don't even need to travel to an office to carry out their duties. Companies can outsource most functions of the business with relative ease. Multimillion dollar corporations are run efficiently by a handful of people. HR management is not only about compensation, benefits and training, but about putting together a nimble, aggressive, sharp team. It can navigate effectively through rapid changes, keep up with innovation and adapt through the generation of new ideas and innovative strategies. A seasoned HR senior manager on your advisory board can bring proven insights and practical assistance to recruiting, developing and retaining strong talent. And that can make a difference to your team.
6) **Research and Development:** Aggressive R&D and constant innovation are an absolute must in today's marketplace. Staying on the cutting edge of technological advances and providing laser-precise solutions in a speedy manner to customers are what keep organizations at the top of their game. You need to make innovation part of your company DNA or growth will be hindered. Access to the latest technical information of your industry is probably available through the Internet. That's true, but it's also available in quantity by the kilo. Your challenge is to discover the true nuggets and pieces of information that will make a difference. In other words, you need insights, not just information. An industry specialist can bring tremendous added value to your team on a part-time basis.
7) **Strategic Intelligence:** Sound strategies will continue to be the key in creating and sustaining healthy growth. In a marketplace where so much specialized knowledge is required to survive and to keep up with the speed of change, the key is the ability to constantly engage in revising and updating strategies. A strategy expert on your advisory board will not only contribute through ideas and innovative strategies, but help you stay alert and keep you focused on the big picture. Many small and medium-size companies lose the balance between the short term and long term by allowing the day-to-day to take most, if not all, their attention. These CEOs and entrepreneurs end up working in their businesses rather than working on their businesses. A senior strategist on your advisory board can help you update your strategy and stay focused on executing it with excellence.

Strong technical experience, a deep understanding of the bottom line and competent managerial skills are simply not enough for success. You have to surround yourself with well-balanced, experienced and qualified board members who possess proven insights in their specific area of expertise and have demonstrated a solid performance record of achieving results. These factors will improve not only your odds of tasting success, but they will help you sustain that success.

When ownership and management are the same, a good advisory board can help protect owners and managers from themselves! When ownership, family and management are intertwined, making the right decisions becomes very difficult. Emotions and family issues inevitably get in the way. An independent and experienced advisory board can bring discipline to the process of making important decisions, especially when strategy is involved. Strategic errors can be very expensive to fix and some errors are fatal.

However, putting together an effective advisory board requires experience and investing in both time and financial resources. Board members must be carefully recruited. You cannot form an advisory board composed of friends and family members. Independence is essential.

Advisory board members must also be adequately remunerated. The board is not a social club, and board members have to dedicate quality time, attend meetings and research subjects in order to function in their role. They are required to do their homework and come to the meetings prepared.

A good advisory board must work well together, but also provide a healthy balance of alternate viewpoints. This creates both harmony and tension for sound decision-making. One other aspect that is important in creating this balance is the advisory board's ability to gain the trust and respect of the senior management team.

An advisory board should be composed of at least five members, two from inside the company (or ownership), and three from outside. After some time (approximately two years), you may increase the board to seven individuals in order to make room for turnover. A board with an odd number is preferred because you are more likely to avoid a tie if the board uses a voting process. The board should meet a minimum of four times a year, and the use of committees can be effective when focusing on particular functions or issues (e.g., finance, HR, R&D, technology, foreign markets, etc.).

Passing on the baton between generations is never easy. But a good advisory board can also help plan and execute a smoother succession plan and/or exit strategy.

Lastly, I would like to underline that while an advisory board is different from a regular board of directors because the directors don't represent different shareholders, it has been my experience to have an advisory board that does almost exactly what a regular board of directors does in terms of responsibilities, meetings, agenda, processes used and voting.

You must give the right sense of responsibility and level of accountability on both sides — the directors and the entrepreneur/president/CEO. Even the voting process elevates the quality of discussion and decision making. The one distinctive difference is that the president (99% of the time is the largest shareholder/owner) has a veto ability to overrule a vote they do not agree with. Obviously, if the president overuses their veto power, the purpose of having an advisory board is defeated.

Private businesses, just like major public corporations, need the best individuals to run things, but the best individuals may not necessarily be the owners of the business. They also need a body that will watch over management to ensure that management is executing its duties skillfully.

I choose to disagree with Arthur Goldberg who once said, "If Columbus had an advisory committee, he would probably still be at the dock." It all depends on Columbus, I say.

Consider creating an advisory board. It may be your secret weapon in achieving success in today's competitive marketplace.

CHAPTER 17

CORPORATE GOVERNANCE

Straight Talk about Corporate Governance and Good Stewardship

"When wealth is lost, nothing is lost;
when health is lost, something is lost;
when character is lost, all is lost."
— Billy Graham

Twenty years ago, when I started my second career by founding my management consulting practice, I predicted that North America would experience a revolution in corporate governance.

When I looked at public corporations that were increasingly owned by large institutional investors, it made sense to me that these institutional investors would want to see good corporate governance practiced by the corporations in their portfolio of investments.

I could see many signs that were not right. Red flags such as excessive executive compensation, stock options that were out of control, large public corporations that were strategically in trouble while the board looked nice and comfortable. All these signs indicated something had to change.

But the years went by and no revolution came. Bits and pieces of corporate governance changes were made here and there, but these changes were limited, to say the least. Then all of a sudden, in 2002, an avalanche of change occurred.

More has been written on corporate governance during the last 10 years than in the previous 20 or 30 combined. More legislation was successfully introduced by the U.S. congress and signed by the U.S. president. These are sweeping changes in corporate law, corporate governance and securities regulation. It only makes sense that Canada was destined to follow suit. However, while legislation is important and necessary, market forces make real change happen.

If you are a director, aspiring director or president of a private company that is considering forming an advisory board or simply interested in corporate governance, pay attention to this section, which summarizes key elements of corporate governance.

The role of the board

While volumes have been written on the subject, here are seven key functions of a board:

1) Review and approve the company (or organization) strategy
2) Monitor the company's performance
3) Authorize compensation
4) Make sure the company complies with all laws and regulations, maintains high integrity regarding financial numbers, adheres to ethical standards and ensures that risks are properly evaluated
5) Provide advice to management
6) Make appropriate recommendations to the shareholders
7) Replace the chief executive officer when needed (this is a bit tricky in situations with advisory boards of private companies)

Raison d'être and primary objective

In a nutshell, the board exists and works to ensure that management is doing a good job. The prime objective of the board is to build, grow and sustain shareholders' value. It is important, however, to know that a board does not come up with a strategy but actually approves management's strategy. The board does not execute the strategy, it only monitors its execution.

Dos and don'ts

Here are a handful of simple do's and don'ts that will apply to pretty well any board and almost any situation. Keep these ten commandments and you will not be disappointed.

1) Two heads are better than one

Have a chairperson and a president. Do not group all the power into one position. All too often, the CEO is the chairman, president, CEO and COO all rolled into one. This is a recipe for feeding inflated egos and for establishing a monarchy, not for running a business. Split the positions of the chairman and the president.

2) Manageable numbers

Keep your board to a manageable number of directors. Seven is a good number. Boards with an excessive number of directors dilute the flow and the potency in favor of administration and routines. If you have a complex or extremely large business, you can always hire external expertise. These experts can provide their opinion or research, but they don't need to be on the board. A large board becomes more of a ceremonial board and costs much more than a seven-person board. It is quality and not quantity you are seeking.

3) Age

Have a good balance of different ages among your directors. Age and wisdom go together, as do youth and new ideas. Boards that have an average age of 75-plus are common, and this can lead to being out of touch. But a board still needs a mix of trendsetters and experience that has weathered many different market conditions.

4) Independence

This is an obvious point; however, so many large public companies would not pass the independence test. Independence has been defined in strange ways lately. Here is what my Funk & Wagnalls dictionary says: "1) Not subject to the authority of another; autonomous. 2) Not dependent on or part of some larger group, system. 3) Not influenced or guided by others. 4) Acting so as to manage one's own affairs; self-reliant." For a board to be productive, you must have independence. A board composed of insiders is not a board but a social club.

It is good for the chairperson to have good communication with board members, but when the chairperson has their friends on the board, that is not good communication. It is a recipe for having a "rubber stamp board," which is a recipe for disaster.

5) Attendance

This seemingly evident point may not always be enforced. What good is it to have the best brains and experience on the board, only to have them absent? Board members must commit to an attendance ratio of 90% or better.

6) Number of boards involvement

As previously mentioned, to do a good job a director must attend 90% of all board meetings and committee meetings. Since they should also dedicate other days to review documentation, read or do research, and review reports and other pertinent information, it would spread them rather thin to sit on several boards at once in addition to their full-time job and other responsibilities. To make things manageable, being involved in a maximum of four boards is optimum. It would also be of interest to casually consider a potential board candidate's commitment to other boards.

7) Conflict of interest

To provide independent opinions and maintain impartiality, directors should not have dual roles. You are either a director or a consultant. You are either the auditor or the consultant, but not both at the same time. Keeping roles streamlined helps maintain the standard of delivery regarding the key functions of a board.

8) Evaluation of the CEO and the board

Although it's a primary role of the board, research indicates that a large number of boards of public corporations do not conduct a CEO evaluation.

An even larger number of boards do not evaluate the board's performance. Yearly evaluations are healthy. They foster open and improved communication and reinforce the accountability factor. Evaluations do not have to be elaborate and admin-intensive. They can be simple, focused and serve as good tools to track results rather than activities.

9) Strategic plans and succession plans

While most corporations have annual budgets, business plans and objectives, many do not have a strategic plan. And if they have one, they fail to keep it updated. The vast majority of companies do not prepare formal succession plans. An updated strategic plan and an updated succession plan are a must for sustained performance. The moment these two documents are out of date, a red flag should come up immediately. These are two crucial tools for the board to appraise management performance.

10) Meetings with and without certain parties

Opinions will vary on this one, but I always recommend that at least one meeting a year be conducted without the CEO. This is not to encourage gossip or blindsiding; on the contrary, it helps to avoid these things by giving directors the opportunity to speak their minds openly at least annually or bi-annually. In addition, I also encourage the board to meet with the auditors without having management present. This way, if any issues are sensitive or there is some disagreement between management and the auditors, the board will hear about it.

Auditors should feel comfortable bringing potentially sensitive issues to the attention of the directors without being criticized by management who may be on the defensive. While most accounting principles and rules are straightforward, some accounting practices can be interpreted differently, depending on conservative or more liberal positions. While there is no right or wrong answer, a meeting with the directors, without management in attendance, provides an opportunity to bring about these issues if they exist. If they do not exist, all the better — the meeting will be quick and less costly.

Most common skills of directors

Directors should be recruited for their skills, experience and talents, and not for their friendship. A strong board can be a tremendous competitive edge for the management team and for the shareholders. A strong and well-balanced board will attract a strong management team. A strong management team will produce high levels of performance. Here are the most common skill mixes:

- Financial experience and knowledge
- Strategic skills
- Sales and marketing experience and know-how
- Human resources expertise
- Technical and production proficiencies
- Information technology skills and capabilities
- Legal expertise
- Experience and knowledge of the global market

The above skills are the core, fundamental skills needed in any board.

By contrast, the following skills are more specialized and may not apply to all organizations: lobbyist talents, academic prowess, R&D expertise, specialized legal know-how, expertise in special categories such as the environment and any other sectors of expertise that apply to your organization's needs.

Selecting directors and the board's chemistry

Selecting directors is a key factor in the success of the board. Not only must the talent bank be rich, but there should be chemistry between board members themselves, and between them and the CEO and the chairperson. Of course, this is easier said than done, but unless the team is flowing together, performance will suffer.

What sets a good orchestra apart is not only the individual dexterity of each player, but the ability of the players to perform as a unit under strong and experienced leadership. Many boards staffed with qualified directors fail to deliver simply because the chemistry is not right.

In private companies, and to a large extent public corporations as well, CEOs prefer to select directors they can trust. If they happen to be close friends, that seems to feel better. If they are also qualified or look qualified on paper, then it appears to be a solid choice. However, while these may seem like good criteria for choosing a board member, these types of actions are motivated by a CEO's desire to have an easy board and to avoid potential criticism and possible conflict.

This is a recipe for failure because a weak board with a "rubber stamp" style will eventually be disastrous to the corporation and ultimately put the shareholders' value at risk. All too often we see examples of public companies that were devastated by incompetent management strategies. Board members who fell asleep at the wheel were indirectly at the root of this incompetence.

As I counsel CEOs of privately held companies to build advisory boards, I encounter hesitance to appoint independent directors. This is because CEOs would instinctively like to select people they can trust as directors. Trust is paramount, but one has to explore their definition of trust. Trust is built on a foundation of high integrity, strong ethics and adherence to high professional standards.

If a CEO makes sure these criteria are present in the board members, trust will be built as they work together. If a director has all the qualifications in the world, but lacks integrity, they are not good candidates. Board members must have integrity beyond reproach and high ethics in everything they do, professionally and personally.

Integrity, ethics and professional conduct are not optional. These are all prerequisites.

While trustworthy people are hard to find, fight the temptation to fill board roles by dipping into your pool of friends and family. Even though a family member or friend may be a co-owner, at some point companies grow to a size where a separation between ownership, management and directors is needed. You can wield more influence by ensuring that you have a strong and well-qualified board in place.

Four steps to recruiting the right board members

First, appraise what your needs are. **Second**, specify the skills, talents and experience you require. **Third**, go find them. Your best choice is to engage a search firm for the selection; a professional search is always a better route even if it will require some investment on your part. **Fourth**, check for the potential chemistry between board members. This could be tested through an informal lunch or dinner, which gives you an opportunity to observe potential board members interact at an informal event or meeting.

When you have completed all four steps, you've completed your task in putting together a powerful and qualified board. Once the board is formed, you must adjust, correct, add, replace, recalibrate and fine-tune as you go along. This will meet fluctuations from various arenas that affect your organization's health and performance.

Good stewardship

Good corporate governance is about good stewardship. It's about the people who have been entrusted with the affairs of the corporation and those who are assigned to oversee the affairs of the corporation. Custodians are given the responsibility of preserving and growing shareholders' value, not the task of getting rich quick.

CHAPTER 18

SUCCESSION PLANNING

"No one plans to fail but many fail to plan. The result is the same."
— Anonymous

Succession planning is a process for identifying and then developing people who have the potential to fill an organization's key business leadership positions. This could be a company, government agency, church or sports team, wherever you have a group of people working towards a specific goal with a long-term focus. Effective succession planning is reached when specific back-up candidates are available for a given position in senior management.

Succession planning in large public companies is usually an important dossier that should be maintained and kept up to date by the board. Strategic planning in private companies tends to be less formal and, in family-owned and family-managed businesses, it may be more complicated due to family relations and the emotions involved.

What is succession planning?

Succession planning is the process by which an organization plans the change of leadership from predecessor to successor. It is the passing of the baton from one leader to another, which is a crucial moment. Any coach will tell you that team relay races are won or lost by how the baton is handed over between runners. Unexpected succession, lack of planning and no practice increases the chance of failure. But good planning and precise execution can improve the odds of making a smooth transition for succession.

Why is succession planning important?

Succession planning is important because it not only influences the performance of an organization but determines its survival. Many companies are destroyed by the lack of succession planning, and many are set back because of poor succession planning.

The CEO role is the most influential role in the organization. Whether we call this position the business owner, the president or the general manager, the CEO is similar to an orchestra conductor. The orchestra conductor may not play any instrument, but they influence the entire orchestral performance and their performance drives the show. Whether the outcome will be a great or mediocre symphony depends largely on how the orchestra is conducted. In business, it's the same. The CEO influences the performance of the entire company.

The CEO influences the strategic momentum and direction of the organization. This person leads the team to higher levels of performance, regardless of how this performance is measured. Increased profitability, revenue growth, attractive return on equity and gains in market share are all performance indicators. The CEO is also in a position to influence the reputation of the organization.

Transitional periods are critical. A change of leadership creates a dynamic where a new balance must be established. Changes implemented by the succeeding leader will require adjustment and getting used to by the entire organization.

Research shows that 70% of private, family-owned businesses do not survive the transition to a second generation, and 90% do not make it to the third generation. These are dismal statistics.

Public corporations don't score any better. These days we are witnessing an unbelievable number of large corporate failures and phenomenal gaffes in succession planning. Poor succession planning is at the root of many business failures. Let's look at some of the issues surrounding this.

When to succession plan

The pace of today's business is fast. The CEO's role should turn over within a reasonable period of time — anywhere between four and eight years. This gives enough time for an incumbent CEO to make a difference, but isn't so short as to project a sense of instability. Any time the tenure of a CEO goes beyond ten years you will find that the risk for potential problems increases. Of course, there are always exceptions to this rule.

As a rule of thumb, I believe that today's organizations need a change at the helm on a more frequent basis. Complacency is a big reason for the decline of a corporation. Over time, ideas and drive become too comfortable, and even the most motivated leader runs out of ideas and fresh points of view.

Another phenomenon is developing a monarch complex. Since good leaders are by nature strong and decisive people, they may be inclined to feel they sit on a throne like a monarch. While a good monarch is a favorable notion, let's keep in mind that monarchical attitudes do not foster the sharing of power with other parties in the organization. They also don't like active boards because a monarchical CEO fundamentally dislikes being accountable.

These two reasons constitute fertile soil for complacency. So many corporations have suffered humbling destinies: market devaluation, the loss of billions of dollars of equity, bankruptcies and marketing defeats at the hands of newcomers. Along with that are corruption, financial debacles and even fraud.

In these examples, the corporations had everything necessary to succeed. What brought about this disastrous outcome? The reason can be attributed to many CEOs who started out as motivated and competent leaders but were unable or reluctant to recognize a healthy time to pass the baton. They slipped into feeling like a monarch at the helm of an organization.

Another reason was most certainly that the board of directors turned a blind eye to the CEO's shift in attitude and fell asleep at the wheel.

Poor succession planning is not only a failure on the part of small organizations, but it occurs in public and private businesses, governments and non-profits.

Consider the following scenario:

A strong leader does a wonderful job. They achieve high performance and get a lot of glory. However, this glory is brief, and the performance must be sustained. The person works hard at putting the wheels in motion to sustain the performance and initially succeeds. Then organizational complacency sets in, accompanied by big egos and a sense of personal ownership. This results in less listening and more directing that takes hold at the top of the organization. Slowly but surely the organization's high performance starts to suffer. In an attempt to save the situation and perhaps save face, the monarch/CEO starts to do whatever it takes to sustain the former glory of the organization.

We have seen this too many times, and unethical and fraudulent methods start to creep in with the sense of desperation on the part of the leadership. It might be in the form of restating earnings, making acquisitions and overpaying for businesses with vanishing equity, building debts that can't be repaid and attempting to fix mistakes by making new ones.

All this is often done with the blessing of the board, which has failed to fulfill its role as a body of advisors and experts dedicated to the organization's well-being. It is only a matter of time before an organization that has fallen into this pattern meets with a breakdown.

Succession planning is an absolute necessity

It is essential for every organization to have a succession plan that will serve them through a transition. Large organizations may have an elaborate succession plan while smaller ones will have a simpler version appropriate for their purposes. A succession plan should be made in advance, and must be well thought through.

When there is no plan or a plan has been hastily put together in a tight time frame, perhaps in response to an emergency, you will often see failure. This failure will have a negative effect on the organization, regardless of its size.

Strategic perspective

Succession planning must also address the strategic context of the organization. This means that if the present leader did a good job turning around the business, the next leader will probably need a different set of skills to build the business. A business with a strong record of consistent earnings growth would benefit from an innovative leader who can take the organization to the next level.

A succession plan must plan for the future rather than copy the past. A common pitfall is when an organization wants to find a leader like the one it had before. Another mistake is when organizations fall in love with the incumbent and don't want to rock the boat for what they perceive to be no reason. This scenario lulls an organization into a false sense of safety. But what they don't realize is that without a healthy succession, the future landscape of the organization will inevitably hit a rocky patch.

A process, not a destination

The search for candidates should take a balanced approach and include looking internally and externally. There are pros and cons for the search for internal vs. external candidates. Good succession plans are not made overnight. They take time to be developed, planned and executed.

Family-owned businesses

A family-owned business that wants to keep it in the family may require a separation between ownership and management of the company. As the business grows, a separation is not only healthy, but desirable.

Expertise, independence and objectivity

It is of paramount importance to seek independent and expert advice. Experts bring to the table wisdom, and the benefit of past trials and errors. External experts also bring objectivity to your organization. When seeking out an expert or consultant, it is worth remembering that **the value of**

advice is in direct relationship to the expertise of the giver and in indirect relationship to the degree of their involvement or interest.

Advisory board

An advisory board made of independent external counselors allows the owner or operator of the business to receive regular business advice and counsel without diluting equity.

The advisory board can then push the organization to excellence by requesting that a strategic plan be made, a succession plan implemented and quantifiable financial targets established. This disciplined approach is certainly helpful in keeping management on track and building shareholder value.

Conflict of interest

All too often, we read about directors who also provide services, auditors who were also consultants and public servants who enjoyed these so-called privileged relationships with third parties. This should be considered a conflict of interest.

Do not compromise on principles. Making exceptions to the fundamental ethics are counterproductive in an organization's quest for success.

Succession planning for senior management positions

Succession planning should also be developed by the head of human resources in collaboration with senior managers. Together they should prepare for an orderly succession for the managers of the organization.

Here is a simple one-page form that summarizes a succession plan:

HR succession plan

Name	
Position	
Start date	
In position since	
Compensation	
Comments	

	Candidate 1	Candidate 2	Candidate 3
Name			
Internal or external			
Start date			
Present position			
Since			
Prior position			
Dates			
Present performance			
Readiness			
Compensation			

Performance: A, B or C (A being the best)

Readiness: 30D (30 days), 90D (90 days), 6M (six months) or 1/2Y (one to two years)

Compensation: salary + bonus + other

A succession plan is a necessity, not an option. Good planning includes a broad outlook, expert advice, common sense, objectivity and business flair. Approach it as a process, and not a destination, and you will pass through the succession minefield safely.

CHAPTER 19

TIME TO SELL THE BUSINESS

"Underpromise and overdeliver."
— Toby Bloomberg

When it is time to move on, there are factors that influence the value of your company.

In large public companies, mergers and acquisitions are familiar ground: They are a way to grow the business through acquisitions rather than organic growth.

In private companies, deciding when to exit the business or pass it on to a different generation of owners can be more complicated. Owners may avoid dealing with succession issues due to their strong attachment to the business. Family-owned businesses may also face conflict that arises amongst family members.

In this chapter we will deal with the many factors that influence business transition and, most importantly, the process of evaluating the worth of your company.

Who is a prospective buyer?

If you want to sell your business or plan a succession, a number of options can be considered. You can sell the business to a family member or members. You can also sell to employees, usually members of the senior management team.

If these two options aren't practical, the most common sale is usually made to an external party, likely a competitor or a company that wants to enter your line of business. This last alternative usually comes in the form of a VC (venture capital company).

This short list of potential buyers should start you thinking about which option is realistic and who your potential buyer is. A buyer who knows your business well, such as a competitor, is usually called a strategic buyer. They are interested in buying your business to strengthen their existing business. They usually take a long-term view. A financial buyer, on the other hand, is usually a VC that is interested in acquiring a company with the objective of raising its value and then flipping it by selling it to a strategic buyer. Their main objective is financial gain.

Strategic buyers are usually better because of their long-term commitment. Though financial buyers are not very friendly and don't have long-term vision, they are normally quick to decide and have ready cash. I am not in favor of one or the other, but simply pointing out the difference.

Valuating your company

Regardless who purchases your company, you need to evaluate the company's worth and determine a realistic price range. A common valuation method used by financial experts is the free cash flow method (FCF).

This valuation is based on the cash that the company is expected to generate in future years. Cash flow is usually the sum of profits and depreciation. You should ask your accountant to help you valuate the company. Alternatively, you may want to engage the services of a firm specializing in valuation.

It is important, however, that you do your homework based on concrete facts and figures. Approaching it this way will minimize making an emotional estimation that may scare off a prospective buyer or underestimate your company's worth. You can also arrive at indicative prices by doing some relatively easy research. Two of the most common methods of valuation are market-to-book-value ratio and earnings-per-share ratio.

Market-to-book-value ratio: Review the market value of public companies that are in the same line of business. The market value is the ongoing price of a share. Compare this price per share to the book value per share. For example, if a share of a certain company is quoted in the market at $45, while the book value of the share is $15, the market is paying a premium of three times book value. If your company's book equity is $5M, applying the same premium (three times) would give your company a value of $15M. While many factors influence this ratio, using the market-to-book ratio gives you a point of reference. (How do you know the book value of a share? Consult the company annual report or use a website that gives the book value per share. Morningstar.com provides this information on all listed stocks free of charge.)

Earnings-per-share-ratio: Find out what the price-earnings ratio is for public companies that have the same activity as your company. If the price-earnings ratio of comparable companies is in the range of 8 to 12 times, and your net profit at the last fiscal year is $1M, then applying the same ratio gives your company a valuation in the range of $8M ($1M x 8) to $12M ($1M x 12). You now have a price range based on a semi-objective method. You can also take the mid-point of the range as a price point. In our example it is $10M ($8M + $12M / 2).

You may also combine different valuation methods by adding them up and dividing them by the number of methods used. For example, you may valuate your company with three different methods. Method A valuates the company at $15M, Method B has a valuation of $10M, and Method C valuates the company at $8M. Which valuation do you use? You may want to add all three valuations and take their average; in our example, the average of the three different valuations is $11M ($15M + $10M + $8M = $ 33M / 3 = $11M).

Using the same example shown earlier, I arrive at a price point of $12.5M. This is done by adding the price point of the first method of valuation ($10M) to the price point of the second method of valuation ($15M), and then dividing by two.

Please note, however, that investing in a small or mid-sized private company is usually considered more risky than buying shares in a publicly owned company. To compensate for this, the valuing of a private company may be adjusted by an appropriate amount that can be called the risk premium.

If a 30% risk premium is applicable, you can adjust the price point we calculated by 30%. Using our previous example, the new price point would be $8.75M ($12.5M – 30% or $12.5M x 0.70).

EBITDA

Another common method is the valuation based on EBITDA multiples. (EBITDA stands for Earnings Before Interest, Tax, Depreciation and Amortization.) Your EBITDA would be calculated for a number of years and then an average is taken. This number would then be multiplied by a certain multiplier for your industry. For example, if your average EBITDA for the last five years was $2M and the multiplier of your industry was a range of five to eight times, then the value of your company would be estimated in the range of $10M (EBITDA x 5) to $16M (EBITDA x 8). You now have a viable figure for pricing your company. Professional valuators will usually adjust the EBITDA valuation by adding or deducting unusual items. What kind of unusual items? It might be compensation of senior managers that are over or under the market level. Or rent that is lower or higher than the ongoing rental market, and so on.

These methods of calculations are straightforward and deliver a relative number that applies to your company's value. Through experience, I have learned that these methods are not a great departure from how professional financial experts reach their conclusions.

Ultimately, valuation methods are more subjective than objective. These methods outlined should not be taken as a substitute for professional valuations, but can serve as a good starting point to find out how much the business is worth.

What to look for?

What factors can increase the valuation of your company? What factors can positively influence the market value of your firm? The following points are essential:

Goodwill and brand name

Goodwill may be classified as an intangible asset by accountants until a buyer agrees to pay a higher value than the book value of the company. Many factors influence the value of a company, but a strong brand is usually an important element of the valuation. Therefore, it is important to invest in and strengthen your brand as a recognizable brand among your customers, which adds to your company's value.

Brand Directory (Brandirectory.com) ranks the top global brands and estimates their value. Not surprisingly, for 2015 the world's number one brand was Apple with a whopping value of $128B, followed by Samsung at $81B and Google at $76B. Not bad for a company that only became public in 2004.

The Google brand is so well recognized worldwide that the name became a verb in its own right as in: "Can you Google it?" Microsoft came in next, followed by Verizon, AT&T, Amazon, GE and Wal-Mart. Coca-Cola, a previous star in the category of brand names, ranked 11th, which is still good for a company that basically sells sugary cola water. IBM came in at number 12.

The bottom line is that possessing a strong brand will likely add significant value to a company's worth. It doesn't matter if the brand is global, national or regional. It just needs wide recognition among consumers or businesses in a designated market.

Concentration of customers

A revenue base derived from a large customer base will command a higher valuation than a revenue base built around a handful of customers.

Let's say that Company A and Company B have similar annual sales volume and a similar number of customers. But company A has 80% of its revenues coming from the top three customers while Company B has its revenues evenly distributed throughout its entire customer base; the valuation of Company B will be much higher than for company A.

This is due to the vulnerability of company A to its three key customers. Losing one of them takes away over a quarter of the revenues, while losing a customer in Company B would be immaterial.

High repeat business

High repeat business from existing customers will usually command a higher valuation. If Company A and Company B have the same sales volume and the same number of customers, but Company A has a business mix of 80/20 repeat customers vs. new customers, and Company B has a ratio of 50/50, Company A would probably have a higher valuation than Company B.

This is because the customers of company A tend to come back again and again, while company B must look for 50% of its yearly revenues from new customers every year. Long-term contracts with customers also indicate steady, stable revenues and, thus, result in a higher valuation.

Strong management team and low employee turnover

A strong management team in place with high seniority and a stable employment level with low turnover are good contributors to a high business valuation. A strong management team with a stable workforce is a good recipe in today's volatile and competitive marketplace where companies compete for qualified human resources and talented managers. For obvious reasons, a workforce that is not unionized will also trigger a higher valuation vs. a unionized workforce.

Trademarks and patents

Businesses with registered trademarks and/or patented products are usually more favorably valuated over firms that don't hold such trademarks and patents. Trademarks and patents are considered a barrier to entry, providing a competitive edge in today's marketplace.

Well-established relationships with key suppliers

Strong relationships with key suppliers and vendors indicate a more stable and durable source of materials. A sturdy and solid supply chain would also be construed as a favorable ingredient in today's marketplace, and would add few points to the business valuation.

Diversification

In some instances, a company with a diversified product/service offering is perceived as a lower-risk proposition and, therefore, commands a higher valuation. In other circumstances, a more specialized and non-diversified product/service company is perceived as a business that is cleaner, simpler and more focused.

This is a double-edged sword because, how could the same subject of diversification be a positive or negative point? A company with a very narrow product line sold only to a handful of customers will be strategically vulnerable to competitors offering a substitute to its one-line product and to reduced demand by a few customers. In such a situation, an enlarged product line and bigger customer base would strengthen the strategic position of the company and its overall valuation.

On the other hand, a company with a very large and diversified product line purchased by a large number of small customers may suffer from the opposite problem. A product line that is too diversified may be easily attacked by an aggressive competitor that offers improved focus on customer needs and improved intimacy with customers who feel lost and underappreciated for their business. In addition, an interested acquirer may find the large diversification discouraging as they may have to resell assets they are not interested in.

It's usually not difficult to figure out if diversification of product/service and customers is a plus or minus. But it is important to know that the level of diversification is a key part to the valuation process of a company.

Smooth earnings and upward trend

There is usually an understandable tendency among buyers to prefer a steady profit growth with a smooth upward slope rather than a series of volatile shifts over a period of years.

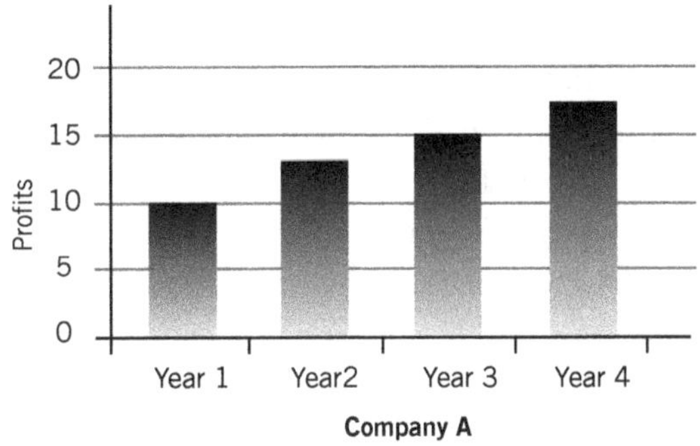

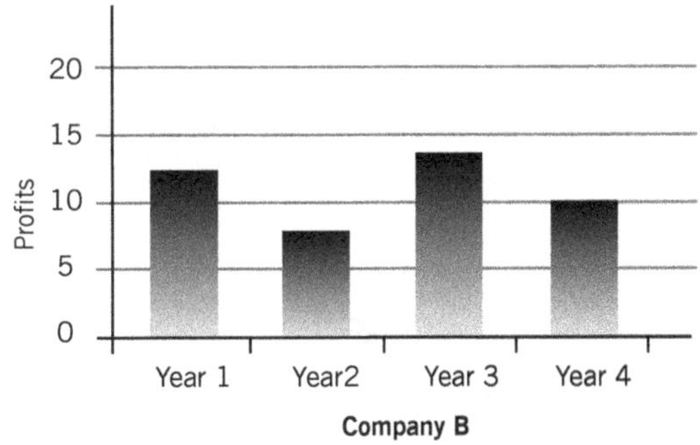

In the figures above, profits made by Company A and Company B for the four-year period are equal. But Company A would probably score a higher valuation because of its consistent upward trend. The same argument applies to the trend for sales, gross profit and equity. Most buyers prefer a consistent upward trend to an inconsistent sales trend.

Exclusivity and market share

It's commonly known that a high market share position allows for a leading role over a certain industry, product, service or geographical area.

Along with leadership comes better control over pricing which, in turn, leads to higher profitability. Exclusivity usually goes hand-in-hand with high market share. In most instances, these two factors usually drive a higher valuation.

Favorable media coverage and a professional website

A track record of favorable media coverage and awards, a leading role in an industry, positive public relations and an attractive website are all positive factors leading to a higher valuation. But the contrary is also true. Ongoing and/or unsettled litigations, negative media coverage and a mediocre website indicate a company with serious issues, and this would lower overall valuation.

Licenses and permits

In some industries or business sectors that require government-issued licenses and permits, or that are regulated by specific laws and regulations, the company holding these permits and licenses can expect to have a few points added to their valuation. This is because of the process needed to obtain these licenses and permits. Government red tape and time also play in favor of companies that already have the required licenses and permits.

Finally, before you embark on a sale, select a team of professionals who can give you good counsel and help you avoid potential pitfalls. Your team should include an accountant, lawyer, business broker and an experienced management consultant.

Many owners and entrepreneurs try to save brokering fees by selling their company directly without the use of an intermediary. I strongly advise the use of a professional intermediary. First, because as a business owner/entrepreneur, you are usually not experienced in acquisition work. You will likely be outgunned by the staff of the acquiring company that is experienced in acquisition work, negotiation and the lengthy process of making a deal. Second, the sale of your company will be emotional, while the acquiring company has performed acquisitions in the past and built experience doing acquisitions. Third, you want to focus on optimizing the 90% to 95% value of the company rather than focusing on saving the 5% to 10% cost of brokering the deal. Finally, while you try to find a suitable buyer for your company, you still have to manage the company. The process of selling the company should not be a major distraction to you or to the performance of your company. But if the sale process drags on for a long period of time, both you and the company may suffer. It's better to leave the non-strategic issues to an intermediary.

Obviously, the choice of the right intermediary is also key to your success in selling the company at the right price and with the right conditions that make the deal a win-win for the acquirer, the seller and all the stakeholders.

The structure of the offer to be prepared by the buyer is important. Not all offers are comparable. Some buyers may offer a higher number up front that suggests a higher valuation, but then you find contingency payments tied to earn-outs or seller financing. This may lead to stretching out payments over a period of time. This is another area where an intermediary can counsel you and highlight the pros and cons of potential offers.

After you spend a lifetime building a family business, deciding to sell is a difficult decision fraught with fears and anxieties linked to the succession process and to the eventual outcome. Conducting good research, planning ahead and surrounding yourself with experienced professionals can turn an emotional decision into a sound business decision and help you achieve your goals for sales and succession.

CHAPTER 20

WORKING SMARTER NOT HARDER

"Working hard and working smart
sometimes can be two different things."
— Byron Dorgan

Here are my ten golden rules for working **smarter not harder**. See for yourself how these ten rules can make your life easier and more productive. If you own your own business, these rules should help you work ***on*** your business, rather than ***in*** your business. They will help you be in control of your business, its direction and its performance rather than being so immersed in the day to day that you are held hostage by the business itself like so many self-employed people who are not enjoying the benefits of being self-employed.

1) The short term vs. the long term

Managing the day-to-day of a business is crucial to the success of any organization, but short-term success does not necessarily mean long-term success. Good short-term results help, but the long-term needs a **strategic plan**. Strategic plans make you think about tomorrow. They answer these key questions: Where are you heading? Where do you want to go and what do you need to do to get there? The importance of planning is vital to your long-term success. **A lack of planning is a plan for failure.**

A lack of a plan can be described as planning for failure simply because if you don't know where you're going, you won't even know when you have lost your way.

Whatever your strategic plan is, it must be the right strategy accompanied by the correct execution. The execution of a wrong plan is just as damaging as having no plan at all. Using the right road map does not guarantee that you will get to your destination, but it will definitely make the job of getting to your destination much easier.

A common mistake is thinking that only large organizations need a strategic plan, and that smaller to medium-size organizations don't. The right strategic plan is essential for the future growth of any organization, regardless of size. The only difference is that large organizations have a more complex plan than a smaller organization.

A good plan must be written down. Plans that exist only in thought or idea aren't plans at all.

No matter how good your plan is, an annual review is needed to keep it relevant and up to date. **The pain of disciplined planning is far better than the pain of regret.** No matter how good your business recipe was in the past, and how many years you have been in business, you must be diligent in setting relevant goals to ensure that you stay ahead in today's fast-paced economy and competitive marketplace.

If the day-to-day is taking all your energy and focus with little or no long-term planning, you are taking a big risk. This is because direction and not intention is determining your destination.

If you are heading in the right direction, your speed will determine when you get to your destination. You can accelerate when conditions are favorable and can slow down when they are not, but you know that you will reach your destination. On the other hand, if you are heading in the wrong direction, your speed is irrelevant. You simply will not reach your destination.

Companies with a strategy are far better equipped as they head toward a certain destination set by their shareholders or owners, as opposed to companies with no strategy that sort of "float around." Companies without a good plan often don't survive, while those with an up-to-date, solid plan are positioned to reach their destination.

2) Excellence in the workplace

Quality work doesn't only lead to higher profits, but it's also a necessary condition for staying in business. Competition is tough. With technology and a global marketplace, your competitors may not be the traditional ones from the past. Also, customers constantly ask for more. In this more demanding and more competitive marketplace, one of your primary objectives must be to seek excellence.

It is worth pointing out that aiming for excellence isn't the same thing as striving for perfection. Striving for perfection may not only frustrate you, but slow down your decision-making process and be counter-productive. **Excellence is your true objective.** Excellence is doing everything to the best of your ability. Seeking excellence means that when you do something, you do it with your best skills, capacity and power.

Let me give you a practical example. A supermarket could have been doing well in the meat, poultry and produce departments, but not as well in the fish department, and still get away with it. At least, that used to be the case. But not today. In today's competitive marketplace, customers simply go elsewhere. They have so many options available to them that you must excel in all departments to win their business.

In the past, customers who wanted to compare prices had to do comprehensive research and visit many stores. Today, they can do all the necessary comparisons and research from the comfort of their homes on various websites that specialize in comparing products, pricing and services. Thus, it is to an organization's benefit to strive for excellence in every section of their business. This will sharpen their competitive edge.

3) Coaching vs. doing

Entrepreneurs, founders and visionaries too often have trouble delegating and coaching. Instead, they prefer to do everything themselves with the thinking that "To get it right, I need to do it myself!" In order for companies to grow and continue to meet the needs of their customers, they must be able to evolve.

There are usually five distinct stages of evolution for entrepreneurs:

1st Stage — The One-Person Band: In this stage the business can be described as being in "start-up" mode. The business is striving for "existence" with an attempt to gain customers and deliver products and service while making a profit.

2nd Stage — Early Success: At this stage the business has demonstrated that it can survive and is workable. Customers keep returning for more products and services. While the organization and the overall business is still simple, it is holding together nicely and scoring some early successes.

3rd Stage — Growing Pains: In this phase the business is expanding and growing, but growth has some pains. Stretching resources always comes with errors, and with any expansion the owner/entrepreneur may have to go outside their traditional comfort zone. As the organization grows, it needs functional managers, and delegation becomes a key component to healthy growth.

4th Stage — People Crunch: In this stage the search for talent is crucial. Also, the need for capital and cash is a key requirement so you can finance the acquisition of human resources (i.e., people who are qualified experienced, and specialized), hence the term "people crunch."

5th Stage – Corporation: The corporation stage is where consolidation and financial gains are realized. The business moves toward a professionally run corporation with better organizational definition, processes, rules, objectives and policies.

It is important to know what stage your organization is in. Knowing this will not only help you pinpoint your evolutionary process, but help you meet the needs of your current level of growth with accuracy and insight.

Reaching the corporation stage requires successful progress throughout the first four stages. There are always variations to these five stages because of your organization's corporate climate, but I have found that these five stages are applicable for most entrepreneurs.

However, some entrepreneurs don't graduate through all the stages. They simply get stuck at one of the stages, and most often it is due to one of two reasons:

a) **Founder's syndrome:** As mentioned, companies must evolve through these five stages of growth so that they can continue to meet the needs of their customers. They need to evolve from an informal entrepreneurial style to a well-planned, correctly managed method of development. But this development cannot occur without first establishing a stable administrative infrastructure. Developing this infrastructure often requires changing the nature of the leadership of the founder. It changes from a highly reactive, individualistic style to a more proactive, consensus-building style. Many founders cannot make this transition. As a result, the organization remains managed, and not in a manner that provides reliable services to customers. It exists according to the personality of the founder.

b) **Coaching:** The entrepreneur's inability to recognize that they need to let go of being a player on the field and become a coach for the team can inhibit moving to the next stage of growth. It is not only about delegating tasks. It also requires creating a team that has a common objective and making sure this team works well together. Here's an example that highlights how this works. A tennis player or a golfer is responsible only for their own performance, unlike a soccer or hockey team, where every player is responsible for their individual performance, as well as the "corporate" performance of the team. In tennis and golf, the coach coaches one person, whereas a soccer or hockey coach must weave together a team with many members. Individual abilities are important, but corporate team performance is the decisive element for success.

One of the greatest tests for entrepreneurs is whether they can make this evolution from player to team coach. As a coach, you switch roles from playing on the field to encouraging, directing and coaching your team's performance from the sidelines.

A similar example is when the first violinist gets promoted to orchestra conductor. They can't play their violin anymore but must direct the entire orchestra. In a similar way, entrepreneurs must learn to move from direct involvement in the job to managing and then from managing to leading.

4) The wisdom of listening to counsel

It is of paramount importance to seek independent, expert advice. Experts bring wisdom and the benefit of having learned from trial and errors. External experts also bring objectivity to your organization. Seeking out and heeding good advice must be one of the key habits for running your business successfully. Strong, successful leaders are often praised for their decision-making abilities, but wise decision-making is rarely a solo performance.

Effective leaders always surround themselves with people who can provide expert and timely information, show the benefit of the information and offer both recommendations and advice about the best action to take.

There is safety in seeking expert, independent advice, and it's important that you pick your advisors carefully. Look for people who have the right experience and qualifications, are trustworthy and can be trusted with confidential information.

Avoid gossipers and angry people with big egos. Independence is also a key factor in choosing the correct advisor. If advice comes only from insiders (i.e., experienced employees and well-meaning friends), these people may compromise by diluting their advice since they may be affected by the decisions. Also, friends don't always have the key expertise required or may not be unbiased in their counsel.

Remember that **the value of advice is in direct relationship to the expertise of the giver, and the value of the advice is indirectly related to the degree of their involvement or interest.**

5) Managing debt and your credit rating

There is a proverb that gives some strong advice: "The poor are ruled by the rich, and those who borrow are slaves of moneylenders" (Proverbs 22:7). As a consultant, I have been privy to the toll that debt can take on companies and individuals. Make it your goal to manage your debt responsibly or, even better, stay out of debt in the first place. "Pay your credit cards every month" is what Regina Brett said. That is good advice. If you need a loan for a large purchase, visit your bank and ask for a credit line, which is usually given at a reasonable interest rate. Do not finance purchases on credit cards because they usually have exorbitant interest rates!

The ability to finance your business through debt is a great privilege and can help you build a successful business, but if you find yourself having to accumulate some debt, ensure that you manage it wisely. In business, don't just look at your profit-and-loss statement, but make sure you also review your balance sheet.

Keep your liquidity high with a healthy and conservative debt-to-worth ratio. Make sure you have adequate working capital. Watch for demand loans that can suddenly be recalled by banks that decide they want to exit your business for whatever reason. Term loans are much better. They are repaid according to a fixed schedule that lets you plan better and pay back over a period of time. There is also the benefit of knowing that as long as you are current with your payment obligation, the lender cannot recall the loan.

Demand loans have no fixed repayment schedule and therefore can be recalled by the bank. This causes the business to scramble in order to pay back the loan in a short period of time, or to look for a different lender altogether. Fixed term loans are friendlier because as long as you repay the loan according to the fixed repayment schedule, bankers cannot recall their loan. While demand loans have some benefits, especially for supplementing your working capital, fixed repayment loans remain a more viable option.

Remember that you can't borrow your way out of debt. If you are taking from one party to pay another, sooner or later it will catch up with you.

Managing your credit rating is also important both for you personally and for your company. Regularly check your credit rating and what the credit rating agencies are saying about you. Ensure that your positive business achievements make it in the credit report. Avoid litigation and disputes by going the extra mile, and by learning to forgive your offenders. Turning the page is not always easy, but is most often a wise decision.

If a business gets into trouble with a heavy debt burden, it will need to dig itself out of the hole. The leadership must be quick to learn from past mistakes and to examine those mistakes so they don't repeat them. An organization's future has no room for the mistakes of the past.

6) Integrity and honesty

Integrity and honesty are subjects that are seldom found on the course curriculum of an educational institution. In my opinion, schools and universities would find it worthwhile to include integrity and honesty on every academic curriculum. The media is riddled with stories about the lack of ethics in business, government, academia, the judiciary or any other sector of society. These reports demonstrate the destructive short-term and long-term effects that a lack of integrity and honesty have on organizations, shareholders, the environment and the public. We can legislate ethical guidelines, but we can't legislate integrity.

Ethics are principles, moral values and beliefs, while integrity is honesty, truth and being upright. Though the gray area does exist, many things in life are really black and white. Compromise is good and helpful in commercial negotiations, but it can't be applied to honesty.

A good leader creates an atmosphere where truth and openness are respected, encouraged and rewarded. If you are in a position of authority and leadership, test yourself to see if you encourage the people under you to be honest, or do you just assume they are? Do they see honesty actively demonstrated in your treatment of them? It is a tough test indeed, but the rewards of living a life of integrity and honesty in everything you do will give you exceptional freedom and strength.

7) Respect your customers

No top ten list of an organization's keys to success would be complete unless we include the role of the customer. If you are in business, you assume that you know the importance and value of the customer. Take a short stroll in the business section at your local bookstore. You will see that more than 1/3 of the business books preach the importance of the customer and effective customer service. So much has been written about honing our customer focus skills, customer care, customer service, customer satisfaction and how to exceed customer expectations.

When it comes to customers, I prefer to use the word "respect." While today's executives and managers know the value and importance of the customer, their hunger for short-term profit and greed often appears stronger than respect for their customers.

Here are three examples that highlight how businesses do not respect their customers:

- On Monday a hardware store has a one-day sale on hammers, and on Wednesday a one-day sale on nails. Why would they do this? It comes across as a ploy to trick the customer. This strategy is set up to bring in the customer for the cheap hammer on Monday, and then get the customer to buy overpriced nails. Then on Wednesday, the store does the reverse by offering a cheap one-day sale for nails, but has overpriced hammers. Wouldn't it be easier for the customer to just have a hammer and nails sale?
- A business advertises a 75% discount. But, in effect, isn't it saying that those particular items are overpriced? I assume they are still making a profit with a 75% discount, so what kind of profit margin are they making on regularly priced merchandise? Another sale offer is "buy two items and get the third one free." Doesn't this tell the customer that they are overpaying for the first two items? A clothing retailer advertises a sale of up to 50% off on selected items, but when you visit the store, you discover that the selected items on sale were low-quality merchandise that you wouldn't wear even if it was free.
- I read this on a bottle of salad dressing which was advertised as Olive Oil and Basil: "This Olive Oil and Basil salad dressing is a marriage of flavors in the pure Mediterranean tradition. It will make you taste the richness of the olive oil delicately elevated with a pinch of basil. A divine association of delicate gastronomy which will amaze your palate for your mixed salads, favorite vegetables and pasta dishes." Wow! Isn't that description great? However, in the list of ingredients, olive oil was only 1.5% of the content! The producer of the salad dressing engaged a writer with excellent marketing skills but will 1.5% of olive oil make me taste the "richness" of olive oil? This doesn't show respect for the intelligence of the customer and, for me, it makes fun of the customer.

These examples highlight a fundamental lack of respect for the customer. In the long term, they are strategies that are self-destructive. I could fill volumes with examples showing disrespect to customers.

Sales and marketing managers should ask themselves the following question: Do I respect my customer? Does my plan for pricing, promotion, advertising and sales and marketing show that I respect my customer?

Here is a very easy way to police yourself: Treat your customer the way you want to be treated.

8) Never give up

In my younger years I used to play soccer, and I would tell the team it doesn't matter how you start the game, it only matters how you finish it. Of course, a good start is ideal, but the principle of never giving up in the face of challenges and obstacles is what brings any project or business through times of adversity. Mistakes are inevitable, but it is imperative that you never give up when you make an error.

Learn from your past, but don't allow yourself or your team to remain captive to the past. Turning the page, moving forward and trying again can be a powerful practice for success. This can be done by focusing on the present, remaining in the moment and planning for the future.

The mavericks of the business world are people who take the time to learn from their mistakes and learn from other people's mistakes. One way to avoid repeating the same mistakes is proactively assessing what went wrong, dissecting mistakes and putting together a sensible plan. The plan includes points of action and points of principle in order to side-step future pitfalls.

Stay ahead of the pack by learning from your own mistakes and the mistakes of others. Swallow your pride and press on to your goal.

A reporter asked a successful banker to reveal the secret of his success. "Very easy," replied the banker. "It is in making the right decisions." The reporter said, "Excellent . . . but, uh . . . how do you make the right decisions?" The banker replied, "Very, very easy — by first making the wrong decisions!"

9) Effective communication

Effective communication is the backbone of successful leadership and the most powerful ingredient for managing with excellence those whom you lead. Whether you are a general manager or GM in training, an executive or an entrepreneur, your success as a leader is largely influenced by your ability to communicate effectively.

Almost any function, position or role requires some kind of leadership, and leadership depends on effective communication. Whether you want to make convincing presentations with confidence, negotiate with ease or resolve conflicts quickly, effective communication is imperative.

The ability to get your message across effectively and clearly is vital. How do you set goals and objectives? How do you communicate with your staff? How do you train, develop, instruct, encourage, correct, lead, present, coach and reward people? These are all crucial components of communication.

10) Balancing life in the fast lane

Technological advances and modern conveniences have turned us into a "microwave society." We talk fast, eat fast, work fast, expect to climb fast and want to get rich quickly. There is nothing wrong with being an achiever, a hard worker and accomplishing great things in a short space of time. Neither is there anything wrong with wanting to advance as soon as possible. However, a good life equilibrium is essential to a happy life, and happiness is the building block to true success.

Life is short and we are only passing through this world. We cannot take any of the wealth, fame and recognition with us. But we can affect the key relationships in our lives and leave a lasting legacy.

If you constantly travel through your life at breakneck speed, you will miss the scenery, and the people who mean the most to you along the way. People work excessive hours on a weekly basis and say that they compensate for those hours with quality time with their spouse and children. While this sounds like a fair compromise, quality time is a misleading concept. Every minute and hour of the day is quality time. Children want to spend time with their parents or parent. Spouses want to spend time together. Visiting Disney World may be a special time, but good quality time can be shopping together, visiting a bakery, enjoying a coffee, walking in the park, visiting friends or jogging in the rain. It isn't what we do or where we go that creates quality time. The deciding factor for genuine quality time is your mere presence. It's showing up and being there that brings life to these activities and destinations.

When you work 50, 60 or more hours a week, you sacrifice so many things. Long-term success doesn't need a big workhorse. Success in business alone will not compensate for the joy of a balanced life. Even if you don't agree with me, I find it difficult to be creative after a 60-hour week! It is impossible to be healthy in body, soul and mind if you constantly work long hours. I am not condoning coasting or doing the bare minimum, because there is great value in going the extra mile. Instead, I am encouraging business people to reach out for balance in everything they do — including work.

Two other important points worth mentioning are the concept of multitasking, and continuous and instant connectability.

I don't know who invented the term multitasking, but this is a recipe for doing things poorly. To do things well, you need to focus and pay proper attention. Doesn't it irritate you when a cashier serves you at the same time he or she is answering the phone or talking with another colleague? When you serve a customer, you look them in the eye and focus on what you are saying. You also listen attentively to what the customer is saying. No multitasking. You make the customer feel important because they are important.

Doesn't it irritate you when people constantly check their smartphone for new emails or messages? This multitasking is not only showing disrespect to whomever you are talking to, but it causes constant distraction.

Today managers are having more difficulty with concentration and being able to differentiate between the important and the urgent. This leads to poor decision-making and disorganization, not to mention being stressed. Multi-tasking is not an ability or a gift. It is a bad habit.

The concept of being "continuously and always connected" is robbing people of their freedom. I receive text messages and emails from people at the strangest hours of the day. Are these people working 24/7? This is frightening! When do people relax? When do they tune off? This constant connectivity is a recipe for stress. Learn to relax and enjoy your free time. Learn to recharge your batteries.

Lastly, as a CEO, GM or entrepreneur in a position of leadership, you need to have your battery charged so you can lead others. With a 60-hour-plus workweek, you're running low or even on empty. This doesn't leave much for you to contribute to a team that looks to you for energy, enthusiasm, strength and innovative solutions. Take the time to seek a balanced life. You will be richly rewarded.

CHAPTER 21

SUSTAINING YOUR BUSINESS PERFORMANCE

> "In business, I look for economic castles protected by unbreachable moats."
> — Warren Buffett

Throughout the previous chapters we reviewed a wide number of subjects, suggestions and actions to make you a better manager. They include strategic planning, business planning, managing costs, human resources, leadership skills, effective communication, teamwork, pricing your products and services, sales management and training. We even covered how to select and manage your banker, lawyer, auditors and consultants. And with the Key Performance Indicators (KPI) we covered how you can monitor your performance and focus on staying the course.

In this chapter, I want to cover how to protect your business performance, and how to sustain your competitive advantage in an ever crowded and more competitive marketplace. As you achieve success and high profitability, your competitors will not sit around to watch you. They will work hard to steal your customers.

Doing more of what you have done in the past and aiming for excellence as I suggested may not be enough to keep competitors at bay. Protecting your business from competitors' attacks requires building business and economic moats around your enterprise. Think of how castles were protected in the past. As you know, a moat is a deep, wide ditch surrounding a castle, fort or town. Typically, it is filled with water and intended to be a first line of defense against intruders and invaders.

How you surround your enterprise and business with a moat is the subject of this chapter. I have identified several sources of moats:

- Building a solid brand
- Intellectual properties (IP)
- Long-term contracts with customers and exclusivity
- Difficult and costly switching costs
- Cost advantage
- Career paths and HR anchors

Value of building moats

Before we discuss these moat makers, I want to underline the incredible value of building moats.

First, a business with a good moat around it will be better valued than one without a moat. Building an effective moat would add a few points of value when you decide to sell or exit the business. This would be particularly attractive to owners and entrepreneurs.

Second, as history has shown, moats are not foolproof against enemy attacks. They serve as a deterrent, usually cause the attacker to suffer more casualties and require more time for the attacker to invade a castle successfully. In business, an economic moat is similar. It won't make you immune to a competitor's attacks but will serve as a deterrent. It should also make it harder for competitors to steal your customers, headhunt your people and/or reproduce your products.

Third, a business moat slows down your attackers just like a minefield in modern military warfare. The enemy can still make it through a minefield, but will lose troops and equipment and, most importantly, time. Time is precious in military strategy and also precious in business warfare, as you will see from my example later.

Building a solid brand

As we have seen in a previous chapter, "Time to Sell the Business," brands are an intangible asset and worth a lot of money. We talked earlier about the leading brands in 2015 with Apple valued at $128B, Samsung at $81B and Google at $76B.[1]

Brands create a business moat around their company. They seal its profits. And their customers do not want to switch brands.

Not only is a brand strong because of its reputation, but brands loved by their customers achieve exceptional competitive advantage for their companies. Consider how Apple is loved by customers who line up overnight waiting for the Apple store to open so they can be the first to get a new product at the launch. Consider how Google is now used as a verb, as in "to Google it," and the legendary brand wars between Coke and Pepsi. A person who becomes a Coke or Pepsi drinker in their youth will most likely continue their loyalty for life.

No matter how small or regional your business is, make sure you invest in building your brand name with customers and within your marketplace. Make them fall in love with your brand, and you will be greatly rewarded in the short-, medium- and long-term.

Brands get created by marketing people, but building a strong brand takes more than a good marketing manager with a good budget. The entire organization must be focused and supportive of the brand and its marketing. In order to be loved, you don't stop at offering benefits to your customers, but you "WOW" them. You make them emotionally tied to your product or service. Remember that you don't inherit a brand and you don't build it by mistake. You work at it and must earn it.

Those who don't invest in brand-building and in strengthening that brand can lose over time. Xerox, Kodak, Encyclopedia Britannica, Oldsmobile and many other strong brands lost their fizz and power over time.

---

1 *Interbrand,* bestglobalbrands.com/2014/ranking (accessed June 10, 2015).

Intellectual property (IP)

Intellectual property, or IP, is a legal term referring to a creation of the mind. The owner(s) of IP are granted exclusive rights. IP includes copyright, patents, industrial design rights, trademarks and trade secrets. IP includes music, literature and artistic works.

IP owners can be an individual, a business or an organization. IP is a form of property. Accountants call this intangible property or intangible assets, but just like brands they can be worth a lot of money.

For example, take the **trademark** of McDonald's, which is a recognizable big M sign with its own design, or the green mermaid of Starbucks. McDonald's is the biggest restaurant company in the world with 36,000 locations in 100 countries, and employing over 400,000 people. Its market capitalization approached $100B in 2015. Starbucks is the biggest roaster, marketer and retailer of specialty coffee with operations in 65 countries, and with a market capitalization in excess of $70B in 2015.

Patents granted to inventors for a limited period of time (usually 20 years) in exchange for a detailed public disclosure of their invention is another form of powerful IP. Nobody can use the same patent unless authorized by the holder of the patent, which might be authorized for commercial use against a license fee. To register a patent, the inventor must meet different requirements including novelty, usefulness and other criteria that differ from country to country.

A **license** or the granting of a license means to give permission to use a patent or to engage in a certain type of activity. Governments or an authority may give a license to allow a particular activity that would otherwise be forbidden. Licenses are usually obtained once the licensee meets certain requirements and pays the appropriate fees.

Think of pharmaceutical companies that generate significant revenues by granting a license to others to produce their drug or medication. They generate profits without the burden of building factories, investments to establish distribution or the headache of running a foreign business. They grant a license and supervise the adherence of the licensee to the terms of the agreement, make sure the licensee maintains the required quality and pays the right licensing fees. What a nice business you say! It's almost like issuing the invoice and accepting the payment!

A company like Walt Disney generated over $2B in its 2013 fiscal from licensing and publishing rights alone.

Having a strong brand may provide you with a marketing moat and give your company a marketing competitor advantage. IP and more specifically trademarks, patents and licenses are an effective form of a moat to protect your product and give you exclusive commercial rights.

Long-term contracts with customers and exclusivity

Another powerful moat is when you have the exclusive right for something. It may be a certain product or service, geographical area, specific license or patent and so on. Common examples include the exclusive distributor of a certain product for a certain market. Customers who would like to purchase a specific brand product must come to you, the authorized distributor in the market. Usually, the exclusive distributor would also provide service, repairs and maintenance.

The practice of engaging customers through long-term contracts can also be a strong moat that protects the relationship from competitors' attacks, at least for the duration of the contract. Long-term contracts are usually given in exchange for a discounted price and/or specific benefits.

An example of exclusivity may include a certain theme park or a restaurant chain that serves only Coca-Cola products. You will find different brands, but they all belong to one company. They can't serve competing brands. This is done through an exclusive contract for a certain number of years. Exclusive contracts almost guarantee a revenue stream for the duration of the contract for both sides of the agreement.

The combination of exclusive contracts, long-term contracts and high-switching costs can result in an "ironclad" moat. Here is a case study in moat building and strategic planning from my experience.

In the mid-1990s, I was the GM of a large marketing research company in Canada. We had exclusive contracts with major food and drug retailers, and with distributors across the country so we could obtain their scanned product data. We gathered the data, cleaned it, analyzed it and then sold it to consumer-packaged goods (CPG) manufacturers. Our information and services provided powerful sales and marketing insights that determined key sensitive, strategic market share information for my clients, along with tactical information for sales distribution.

A U.S. competitor who wanted to invade the market could not obtain the same data since our contracts were exclusive. The competitor convinced the Competition Bureau of Canada (CBC) that we had cornered the market with these exclusive contracts, which meant they could not enter the Canadian market. The CBC came after us to abandon these exclusive contracts to allow fair competition. CBC argued that we had 100% of the market for scanned data in Canada and, in doing so, had created a monopoly. But we had not created a monopoly. We had built an economic moat around our business. We argued that the definition of the market was very narrow. We were trying to enlarge the definition of the market to include general market research, while they were narrowing the definition to scanned data.

Realizing that we were not going to win, based on the defense of a market-size definition, we decided to engage in a different strategy. It was a stretching game. We argued this for a whole year to give us time to build a new and different moat around the business.

While the lawyers argued for a year about market definitions, legal matters, fair trade practices, etc., we were busy digging our new moat by signing new non-exclusive contracts with retailers and distributors. The difference, however, was that these long-term contracts had different dates and durations. Many of them had service components, and not only money was involved.

We also got busy signing up clients (the CPG companies) with multi-year contracts and offered them discounts and customized services. These contracts carried different dates; some were for one year, some for two and some for longer periods. Having done that, we rolled over to the CBC and agreed to dismantle and abandon our old exclusive contracts. The CBC was happy, our competitor was happy, and we were happy that all ended well!

Our competitor then approached retailers and distributors for their scanning data. While the data was available for sale, its price was now exorbitant, and our competitor could not come up with the services we had introduced. Approaching the customers with their potential services to be launched was also next to mission impossible since customers had entered into long-term contracts with us and did not want to give up their new customized services. Their switching cost was high and certainly not worth whatever the competitor could offer them.

Our competitor realized too late that both doors were closed: Retailers would sell their data at a very high price and customers were not willing to switch suppliers. Our new strategy had created an even stronger, deeper moat. The competitor tried to approach the CBC again, crying wolf, but this time the CBC could not find anything illegal with our commercial agreements. We had simply built a new legal and sound moat around our business. By the way, this moat that was built in the mid 1990s is still keeping this competitor and others out of the market. Twenty years later, the moat is still working!

When you combine exclusive contracts and/or long-term contracts and put in place high-switching costs, it can result in a very powerful moat that protects your castle.

Cost advantage

Cost advantages give you the ability to be the cost leader, which can then be transferred to being the market leader. Wal-Mart is a great example of how a cost advantage lets you become a market leader. Wal-Mart's efficiency with procurement and logistics processes allows it to offer lower prices that appeal to a large number of consumers. Walmart is the biggest global retailer with sales approaching $500B annually, with 11,000 stores and two million employees worldwide.

When you have a cost advantage, you have improved control over pricing, and with improved control over pricing you have improved control over profitability. It's as simple as that.

Cost advantage can come from higher productivity, procurement and logistics efficiency, best practices manufacturing and proficiency in sales and marketing.

Leveraging cost advantage can also be a marketing strategy for timely territorial advantage. For example, a big retailer is invading a new rural market and will compete with two small local retailers. The newcomer may reduce the price of the top 50 grocery items, so the two locals match the price to keep customers. But, after a while the big retailer reduces the price even more, and with the two locals matching it this price war cannot be sustained by the two local players. Ultimately they abandon and fold. Once they are out, the big player increases the prices.

The small retailers had only one strategic defense. Their hope for survival was a differentiation strategy, not a price-war strategy, which is based on a cost advantage for the big retailer. You may call this a marketing price war or a cost advantage war. Either way, it highlights the tremendous effectiveness of the cost-advantage moat.

Career path and HR anchors

A lesser-known moat involves protecting your key players and senior team members from the poaching of competitors. Competitors can copy your business in one way or another. They can buy the same machinery and equipment, purchase from the same suppliers, open similar stores or branches, match your prices, copy your service and so on. They can even try to hire your people. What they cannot duplicate is your team, your values and your culture.

For sure, they will try to copy these, too. But they will not be able to live them, and the intrinsic power in your team, your company core values and your company culture cannot be easily duplicated.

Sometimes people can look alike. Twins come very close to almost being a perfect duplication, but no one of seven billion people in the world has your fingerprint, and no one has the same iris as you do. Each one of us is unique. There is only one of you and one of me. In the same way, there is only one team. Make it unique, personal and special.

Now, even with your team, make sure you build a moat around your individual players. You do that by first getting to know them individually, and by getting to know their passions, needs and desires. What turns them on and what turns them off? Get to know their gifts and their talents. Then, build with them a career path for the short and long term.

Together you, them and the team can build the enterprise and achieve their professional and personal goals. It's a win-win approach.

I recommend giving these people an interest in the enterprise, if appropriate. It could be a minority interest, but look at companies that offer their employees ownership plans. You notice their superior HR resources in high productivity, high quality, pride of belonging, innovation, high engagement, service excellence, customer satisfaction, employee loyalty and, most importantly, solid bottom-line performance.

Money matters are not the only tool for making HR anchors. There are many tools at your disposal for anchoring your star performers, senior team members and your people in general. These include clear objectives, good training, meaningful feedback, a sense that their work matters, a fair reward, a benefit program, recognition for performance and a team spirit. The list is long.

People like to belong and shine when they are engaged and recognized. Engagement and recognition go beyond respect. This higher level of HR can give you a decisive moat and a significant competitive edge.

To summarize, I have covered five different buckets of moat enablers with many types within each bucket: building a strong brand to differentiate your marketing offering and make customers love you, surrounding your product with IP instruments, offering your customers commercial options to protect them from competitors' attacks, managing your costs wisely and anchoring your star players/key people and HR resources for the long term.

One last comment. While we are on the subject of the economic and business moat, you achieve success as a business when your profits not only exceed your accounting costs, but exceed your investors' opportunity costs or, in other words, their opportunity to switch their investments somewhere else. Why would you stay in business if you can generate with your capital a much higher and less risky return somewhere else?

If you neglect to build moats in a free-market economy, competitors will eventually try to take your profits away. Moat building will give you a better chance to protect your present and your future.

CHAPTER 22

BACK TO BASICS

Managing Your Receivables and Your Inventory

"The difference between who you are
and who you want to be is what you do."
— Anonymous

This may sound too simplistic, but after completing over 350 consulting assignments during the last 19 years or so, I can say that at least 200 of the CEOs and entrepreneurs I worked with should read this chapter.

Accounts receivable (A/R) and inventory are, by far, two of the largest asset categories for most businesses. This is especially so for manufacturers, wholesalers and many B2B service providers. Yet these two types of assets are usually not managed well and have much room for improvement. So, with that in mind, here are some very practical and down-to-earth suggestions that will make you "best in class" for managing your accounts receivable and inventory.

Collecting your accounts receivable and establishing credit controls

This is a short summary of the basic rules for collecting your A/R promptly. If you follow these simple instructions, you should be able to achieve

significant improvement in the collection of your A/R and a reduction of your bad debts.

While the type of customers and the type of industry influence your credit and collection performance, my experience convinces me that 90% of the time your performance in collecting receivables **depends more on what you do** rather than on what your customers do. If you extend credit, then you make the rules. It does not matter if you are a big or a small company. Of course, you will be influenced by the norms of your industry, but you should always aim to be the best in your field.

1) RESPONSIBILITY

Give the responsibility of the credit and collection function to *one person* in your company. One person must be accountable. That person should have ownership of the collection of A/R. They should be trained and must work well on the telephone, make good use of emails and possess good communication skills. They should know how to strike a balance between being courteous and friendly, and firm and disciplined. The person should be good with numbers and well organized. Finally, they should take pride in their job and enjoy it!

This one-person recipe should apply to most small and medium-size businesses. Obviously, if your company is big and the workload can't be managed by one person, you should have a team headed by a credit manager.

2) What is our MISSION? And what do we do with new customers?

Here is an example of a mission and simple rules: The credit department is responsible for maintaining a high quality of accounts receivable, while selling to all customers who are acceptable credit risks. We will provide flexible mechanisms to protect our substantial receivable investment. (You can have a liberal or conservative credit policy, but you should always demand prompt A/R and very little in credit losses.)

The credit department is responsible for collecting our investment in A/R. It is our responsibility to take no unwarranted risk, and to see that payments are made within terms. We will advise our sales department about customers who represent risk situations and make efforts to limit our credit exposure in these areas.

If you agree with this description, then **all new customers must be checked for their credit worthiness**. Some companies depend on internal sources (sales force, gut feel, filling of credit application, calling of references) and others depend on external sources (obtaining a credit report, attending credit round table, etc.) or a combination. Whatever you do, do it consistently and appoint one person to take on the responsibility for approving and extending credit.

3) What are our GOALS?

Define your goals. Here is a short list of practical objectives:

- Our goals are to limit bad debts to ____ % of sales (e.g., 0.5%, 1%, 2%, etc.)
- Our day sales outstanding objective is ____ days (e.g., 30 days, 45 days, 60 days, etc.)
- Our receivable aging objective is no more than ____ % beyond 60 days (e.g., 10%, 20%, 30%, etc.)
- Past due customers will be contacted by telephone within ____ hours/ days (e.g., 48 hours, 36 hours, 2 days, 5 days, etc.)

How to calculate the average collection period:

Accts receivable / annual sales x 365 days = ANSWER in days
Example: Accounts receivable $250,000 and annual sales $1,500,000.
$250,000 / $1,500,000 x 365 = 61 days

4) PROMPT INVOICING and CLEAR TERMS OF SALE

Make sure that invoicing is done promptly every week. Don't wait for month-end. We do not need to wait many days to send our invoice. The faster we invoice, the faster we collect. We should also make sure that there are no "misunderstandings" about our terms, e.g., due upon receipt, net 30 days, etc. There should be no confusion whatever about when payment is due!

5) WHO IS THE ACCOUNTS/PAYABLE (A/P) CLERK for our CUSTOMER?

We should know who is in charge of A/P at our customer and have their name, position, telephone number and email address. We should know who to talk to when our invoice has not been paid, and who to thank when it is paid. We should establish a good rapport with them and always stay in contact. It doesn't matter how big our customer is, and how computerized their A/P process is. There is always a human being at the other end who is responsible for A/P. We need to know this person well. We should keep this up to date for all customers.

6) Establishing a CREDIT LIMIT for every customer

It is a good policy to establish a credit limit for every customer. The limit can be established with help from a credit rating company, or with the financial manager or credit manager. Credit limits should be based on the ability of the customer to pay, and on our own credit risk. Customers should first demonstrate that they pay on time before their limit is raised. Credit limits should be updated regularly, and big clients should have their limits established and approved by a senior manager in your organization.

7) Calling customers when they are past due

All customers should be called when they are past due. The sooner the better. The person in charge of credit and collection will then supplement the calls with emails and letters, as the situation warrants. The salespeople should be informed and should help in the collection process, as need be. Salespeople should get involved when the credit and collection person has already initiated a collection process that did not bring positive results. Not before. At the same time, they should not be notified when everything else has failed. In other words, not too early and not too late. How early and how late need to be agreed upon. All staff should be reminded that this is a team effort.

8) SET CLEAR and CONSISTENT PROCEDURES

Good organization and a disciplined and consistent process are key to successful collection of A/R. For example, set specific days and times to invoice (e.g., Tuesday afternoon and Thursday afternoon at 2 p.m. are set for invoicing. Check all A/R for past dues on Wednesday morning before noon and make the first telephone calls on Wednesday afternoon). Follow-ups should be entered into your TASKS for the week/day on your Microsoft Outlook (or similar online system) so that when the A/R clerk arrives in the morning, they can handle follow-up calls scheduled for the day.

9) AGING OF RECEIVABLES

This report is usually available from the list of accounting reports, which in turn come from the reports menu of all accounting systems. The report should be reviewed at least twice a month. For example, it could be on the 2nd and the 15th day of the month. Look for large past dues and handle them with urgency. Look for repeat offenders. Consult with the sales manager and the financial manager for alternate ways of handling a special account.

10) SAMPLE LETTERS/emails

If you need to send letters/emails to remind customers of their past due, here are two samples:

a) Your payment of [AMOUNT OWED] pursuant to our invoice dated [INVOICE DATE] has not arrived by the date required. We are sure that this is an oversight and ask that you please send your check today. (If by letter add "in the enclosed self-addressed envelope" and enclose a self-addressed envelope.) If you have already sent your payment to us, please accept our thanks. If you have any questions, please feel free to call the undersigned at [YOUR COMPANY'S PHONE NUMBER].

b) This is our second reminder that payment on your account in the amount of [AMOUNT] is due on [DATE] is still outstanding. We value your business and hope to keep you as a customer. However, we do require payment according to the terms of our invoices. Please send us your payment today.

The collection method that is the most appropriate and cost-effective for each circumstance will depend on many factors. Please note, however, that sending letters or emails does not substitute for telephone calls. Telephone calls, letters and emails complement each other and help you collect your A/R promptly.

If all your collection actions failed, consider using a collection agency or a specialized lawyer. This last resort should be the exception rather than the rule, and will usually result in the loss of customer goodwill.

Customers not paying on time can be attributed to one of two reasons: their willingness or their ability. If it is their ability (i.e., they want to pay, but don't have the money), manage this by agreeing with them on a repayment schedule (i.e., a temporary arrangement until they are in a better position). But, if the customer is not willing to pay, then the sooner you involve a collection agency or lawyer (for a legal process), the better your chances of collection.

Collection procedures and actions are usually based on the methods and information outlined above. I again underline the importance of organization, consistency, clear communication and routine processes with a built-in progression to more complex procedures as the situation warrants. HAPPY COLLECTION!

Managing your inventory

Similar to your A/R, the inventory is one of the largest categories of assets on your balance sheet. The way you manage your inventory is key to your customer satisfaction, to supporting your sales force and, most importantly, to a healthy bottom line.

Managing your inventory and your profitability

Let's start with a simple example that demonstrates the importance of your inventory turnover and how it influences your bottom line.

Shown below is an example of three companies that have three different levels of profitability in terms of gross margin, but all three sell their product at the same price.

Company A buys its product for $50 and sells it for $100, making a gross profit of $50 or an attractive gross margin of 50%. Company B buys its product for $70 and sells it for $100 (same as Company A), making a gross profit of $30 or a respectable gross margin of 30%. But it's still 20 points less than Company A. Company C buys its product for $80 and sells it for $100 (same as Companies A and B), making a gross profit of $20 or an OK gross margin of 20%, which is a full 30 points less than Company A and 10 points less than Company B.

The big difference between the three companies is that Company A turns its inventory three times a year (once every four months), while Company B turns it inventory six times a year (once every two months) and Company C turns its inventory 12 times a year (once a month). While all three were selling at the same price, after one year Company C has sales of $1,200, Company B sales of $600 and Company C sales of only $300. Company A made a profit of $150, Company B a profit of $180 and Company C a profit of $ 240! *Company C, with a significant lower gross margin, achieved over 60% better profit than Company A and over 30% better than Company B.*

	Company A	Company B	Company C
Sales (Price)	$100	$100	$100
Cost	$50	$70	$80
Profit	$50	$30	$20
Number of Turns	3 (every 4 months)	6 (every 2 months)	12 (every month)
Yearly Sales	$300	$600	$1,200
Yearly Profit	$150	$180	$240

The moral of the story is that inventory turnover is key to your profitability. Watching your P&L and maximizing your mark-up are important, but **inventory turnover is the real driver of profitability**.

In our example, Company A had the best mark-up and the highest gross margin but was the least profitable. Don't get stuck on the P&L level. Manage your inventory turns!

Now that I have your attention, let's look at ten easy ways to better manage your inventory:

1) RESPONSIBILITY

Like my first suggestion with A/R, give the responsibility of inventory management to *one person* in your company. One person must be accountable. The person should have ownership of the inventory level and mix. The level of inventory refers simply to the value of the total inventory, and the mix to the various parts or items of inventory, which are most commonly referred to as SKUs.

SKU (stock-keeping unit) identifies a particular product and allows it to be tracked for inventory purposes. Typically, an SKU is associated with any purchasable item in a store or catalog.

This person should be trained and must know your product line. They must be familiar with the origin of products and their vendors, and possess good communication skills so they can work with your sales manager and sales force. The person should know how to strike a balance between responding to customers' needs and requests, and maintaining the overall inventory level at the desired level of investment. The person should be good with numbers and well organized. Finally, they should take pride in their job and enjoy it!

This one-person recipe should apply to most small and medium-size businesses. Obviously, if your company is big and the workload cannot be managed by one person, you should have a team headed by one manager.

2) Intelligent classification of inventory

Classify products, items and SKUs in many ways. Here is my favorite list of classifications:

a) **By categories:** Classify the inventory in 8 to 12 large categories or less. Resist the temptation to go beyond 8 or 12 by using subcategories. You want to see the "big picture" before you jump into the details. For example, a grocery store would look at various departments such as meat, fish, fresh produce, dairy, bakery, CPG (consumer packaged goods), health and beauty and household. A shoe retailer may look at his inventory in categories in terms of men, women, children, dress, casual, sport, boots, bags, shoe accessories, etc.

b) **By contribution to sales:** In this classification organize inventory by its contribution to overall sales (revenues) so as to manage the categories and the products mix with the right priorities. This gives more importance to the items or SKUs that contribute a greater portion of sales. This classification has nothing to do with sales opportunities. It simply gives proper attention to the items that contribute more to revenues.

c) **By vendor/supplier:** Knowing how much we buy from each vendor/supplier will help us evaluate our reliance on key vendors and suppliers, as well as give us an opportunity to manage our purchasing on better terms.

d) **By mark-up and gross margin:** With this classification, we grade our inventory mix by the contribution of items/SKUs to our profitability as expressed by gross profit. Like our comments on the sales mix, this classification has nothing to do with sales opportunities. It simply gives proper attention to the items that contribute more to our profits.

e) **By time needed to deliver product from our vendor:** When deciding how many items to stock of a particular product (or SKU), consider the time it takes to replenish, and how long you must wait to get the item delivered. If we can get this item or product delivered in 24–48 hours, we can correct our out-of-stock situation promptly, but if it takes three weeks to get the item/product, then we should be more conservative and stock enough of it to reduce the likelihood of being out of stock!

3) Classification of A, B, C and N products

Classify inventory on the basis of four categories with A items/SKUs being those that contribute the largest amount of sales. This will vary from one company to another (i.e., it could be 80% for one company, 70% for another and 60% for a third). B category is for the secondary portion and C is for a third portion. For example, A category is for items that contribute 70% of total sales, B category for items that contribute 20% of sales and category C for items that contribute 10% of sales. The N category is reserved for new items/SKUs added for a period of time (i.e., first 6 months or 12 months of launch of new products) until we get a better control over customers' demand. After a certain period of time, items classified as N should now be reclassified as A, B or C. A fifth category, O (for obsolete), may be added as items you used to carry and are now delisted/dropped.

4) Quarterly review

Once a quarter, review the list of the top XX items/SKUs and the bottom ones. The purpose is to make sure that all top items have been classified as A category and that we are providing the right sales and marketing attention to them. The bottom items may be delisted from our regular inventory or sold via a special sale to get rid of them. The quarterly review meeting and analysis should be done jointly with the sales manager, operations manager and financial manager, along with the manager in charge of inventory.

5) Establish internal objectives

Establish internal objectives for order fulfillment, out of stocks, open orders, inventory levels by quarter, etc. These objectives will provide clear measures for managing inventory optimally. Without set objectives, salespeople will have you stock every possible item in great quantities, and if financial people are in charge, you will have the absolute minimum in inventory. I may be exaggerating, but my point is that you need to have a good balance between satisfying your customer needs and keeping inventory at reasonable levels and to make an honest profit.

Here are example of objectives:

- 80% of orders must ship within 48 hours of receipt
- Products A should never be out of stock
- Warehouse costs should be less than 2% of sales
- Back orders should not exceed 5% of sales in value
- Out of stock should not affect more than XX customers at any point in time

6) Obsolete items/SKUs

Once items have been identified as obsolete items/SKUs, you need to have them removed through a clear, consistent process. There's no point carrying these items/SKUs because they represent "idle cash" and their absence will not affect customer satisfaction. You may decide to have a special sale at an attractive discount or identify a specialized vendor who can purchase all of them at a discounted price. Some companies specialize in out-of-stock items or obsolete items/SKUs. Whether you decide on your own "fire sale" or using a specific channel, the important point is that you continually and systematically cleanse your inventory from obsolete products/items/SKUs.

7) Minimum two vendors for each item/SKUs

It's good to always have a choice between two vendors — preferably three — for every item or SKU in your inventory. This allows you to compare prices, service, deliveries, etc., while also reducing your vulnerability to a specific vendor/supplier.

8) GUARANTEES and WARRANTIES

If you offer guarantees or warranties, make sure items and SKUs related to these special offerings are clearly identified so your inventory can respond adequately to customer requests and needs.

9) Well-organized warehouse

Have a well-organized warehouse with clear and visible labels and signage. That means unique, short and unmistakable item numbers and products/SKU descriptions. This will contribute to best practices for inventory management. The success of Wal-Mart is attributable to many things, including selling at low prices and strict procurement policies of always going to the source and avoiding the middleman. But much of its success stems from strong logistical systems, including inventory management. Another example of very advanced inventory management is Amazon, which ships items sometimes in almost real-time. Amazon is known for exceptional order-fulfilling capabilities and computerized inventory-and-management systems.

10) Inventory software systems

Following along from point 9, investing in a good inventory software system is key to your success. A system that tracks all inventory activity, allows many users to access the system and provides accurate historic and real-time analysis and insights can be a superb competitive tool. It will improve your ability to serve customers well, while keeping inventory at optimum levels. The ability to accurately forecast customer needs can also give you an engine of sales growth and prove to be a competitive edge.

It goes without saying that you must do good due diligence on your choice of systems. Calling existing customers about the system will usually give you an excellent insider opinion, not only about system capabilities and benefits, but also other information like flexibility, ease of use, training, time to install, ability to handle special needs, customization requirements and ongoing maintenance. When purchasing systems developed in foreign countries, make sure that the system can handle local and domestic requirements. This may include tax consideration, language needs and speed of Internet connections.

CHAPTER 23

SYMPTOMS AND DIRECTION

"Resting on your laurels is as dangerous
as resting when you are walking in the snow.
You doze off and die in your sleep."
— Ludwig Wittgenstein

In this last chapter of *Maverick Leadership*©, I want to share some final thoughts and discuss two key issues. These two things could potentially "trump" all your good work and prevent you from implementing everything we discussed in previous chapters.

Recognizing symptoms

The first issue, and one of the biggest mistakes managers make, is to *try to fix symptoms rather than address the root cause of the challenges/obstacles they face.* Always go to the root, the real issue, or source of the challenge.

Here are some common challenges that managers face:

- Sales are up, but profits are down
- Sales are up, but you are losing customers and market share
- There is no time to plan
- Your company provides a long list of employee benefits, but everybody appears stressed and crisis management is the norm
- You are paying above-market compensation, but unforced turnover is high and employees are not motivated

Do any of these statements apply to your company? If yes, then read on . . .

These statements summarize specific needs and issues that require rapid intervention and solutions. If left unattended, they will cripple your business and lead to failure. It doesn't matter if it's a large or small business, private or public, entrepreneur or family-run enterprise. What matters is finding a solution that can fix these challenges.

Consider the following big-business failures and bankruptcies:

General Motors. In 2008 GM had $90B in assets and 245,000 employees. It had plants in 34 countries and sold cars in over 100 countries!

Eaton's. This major Canadian department store, a retail icon, was founded in 1869 and grew to 70,000 employees. In 1999 it filed for bankruptcy.

More recently, **Target**, a large U.S. public company and one of that country's biggest department stores, launched its entry into the Canadian market by opening 130 stores. It was a huge investment. But in less than two years it had to close its doors. In 2014 and 2015, Target showed losses of over $1B. Its slogan was: "Expect more, pay less. Target loves Canada."

I am using these bankruptcies as examples of large companies that had everything for success. They had a strong brand name, capital, goodwill, resources, assets, locations, credit, experience, etc. — all the components needed to succeed. Just as important, they had the ability to acquire the resources and expertise to resolve any problems and challenges.

Why did these companies fail? In my opinion, two reasons.

1) Don't only deal with the symptoms

First, they failed because they dealt with the symptoms and *not* the real issues. You must diagnose correctly *before* you start the fixing.

They failed because their executive team pursued the wrong strategy and their board was asleep at the switch. Consider the following:

The CEO of **GM** traveled to Washington, D.C., in a private corporate jet to ask for help from the U.S. government! This would be like me showing up at your door coming out of a stretch limousine and begging for money! No matter how good you think your strategy is, and how big and important you think you are, you have to look at the results. An executive team that has been delivering poor results for some time needs to be changed. To succeed in business, you need strong teamwork. You also need humility and modesty. This allows you to listen to advice when your way of doing business does not bring the right outcome.

The same is applicable to **Target**, which assumed that its U.S. success only had to be duplicated in Canada. Not doing your homework on a new market and not listening to advice is a sign of arrogance. When you think you know it all, you take a big risk. In today's competitive marketplace with all those demanding customers, you must partner with your customers and also with your employees, suppliers and shareholders. You need to work on WIN-WIN relationships. It's sheer fantasy when executives and board members think large size makes them invincible in business.

As reported in the press, the Target failure was caused by five reasons:

1) Empty shelves
2) Canadian shopping habits
3) High prices
4) Intense competition
5) No online presence

While these are all valid points, I think of them as symptoms that could easily be corrected. Empty shelves can be fixed with good logistics. Adjusting to new shopping habits requires research. High prices can be lowered. Knowing your competitive landscape is Business 101, and an online presence is a key marketing tool in today's marketplace. These are five ABCs of modern retailing. How could a successful department store miss them? As I say, these are symptoms. The real roots are a lack of strategy, arrogant management with an attitude of knowing it all and a board that is asleep.

How about the failure of **Eaton's**? The infighting of family members created disagreement at the top of the organization. There was no team play. As I said in previous chapters, the importance of team play and the need to align all company resources are key to business success in today's market. Employee engagement at all levels is the crucial ingredient for standing out in a competitive marketplace.

Today's customer has access to many tools and is well informed. Customers have so many options. If you don't give them a good reason to choose your product or service, they can easily go elsewhere.

Never cover an error with another error. Don't stop at addressing the symptoms. Always attack the real root of the problem. And attacking the real root of the problem may require more time and resources. That's fine, but don't stop with a "duct tape" solution because in time the duct tape will give up and you will revisit the same problem. Chances are that the problem will be even greater.

2) Direction is key

The second big mistake managers make is failing to get their direction right. Make sure you are heading in the right direction. Speed will come later on. Your direction is key.

As I said in a previous chapter, you can drive a Ferrari at full speed, but if you're heading in the wrong direction, you will never reach your destination. Even a bicycle going in the right direction will beat you! It's like the tortoise and the hare.

I was recently in a big shopping mall in Toronto. A store that had been occupied by Target was sitting empty. While the Target name had been erased from the building, the company's huge red cement balls were still displayed at the entrance of the store. But Target had vacated the store a year earlier! Why didn't Target remove the red balls? These red balls are a symbol for the Target brand. How could they leave these behind? Did it save money? Or didn't they care? This tells me that the management team didn't learn its lesson. After such a disastrous entry and exit into and out of the Canadian market, senior management remained arrogant and unrepentant.

The Canadian failure of Target led to the closure of 133 stores, the loss of employment for 17,600 employees and in Q4-2014 some $5.4B in pre-tax losses on discontinued operations.

Still on the subject of direction, remember that strategic missteps always take a long time to fix or reverse. Tactical missteps are easier to correct, and operational errors can usually be fixed rapidly. In other words, tactical and operational errors can be fixed faster and with modest resources, while strategic errors can be fatal and will usually require significant resources and more time to fix.

So, if sales are up but profits are down, don't keep making more sales. First, find out why profits are down. Is it because of pricing? Are costs out of control? Is productivity down? Or is it due to sloppy quality or poor management? You must find the real problem.

If there is no time to plan, ask why? Do you have the right leaders? Is the board asleep? The short term is important, but long-term success needs long-term planning. If you pay people well and offer a good benefits package, why are they stressed and always in crisis mode? Do you have the right management team? Are you promoting work-life balance or are you running a sweatshop? Are you promoting employee engagement? Are you really living your values or just talking about them?

Today's successful business needs to create an environment that allows people to excel at work, while also having a balanced life outside work. Engaged employees mean happy employees, and happy employees mean happy customers, and happy customers mean good profits and that means sustained success.

I might be oversimplifying things, but get your ABCs right, get your basic foundation right and your main direction right *before* you jump into execution mode. Neglecting the real root of the problems and not making sure your direction is right will almost always defeat your best efforts.

You may think that I am oversimplifying things. So I would like to share with you some personal observations and real stories that happened to me. They show that simplifying things does work!

You have heard the old saying "a fish rots from the head down." When an organization, company or state fails, leadership is usually the root cause. Who represents the head of the corporation? The senior executives and the board.

CEO of the year!

A few years back I was visiting Washington, D.C., to attend a three-day annual meeting of an important professional association. For the event, the association had invited the CEO of a major public company. Their CEO was elected CEO of the year. Since I owned few shares of the company, I wanted to meet the CEO in person. What a disappointment. He was arrogant, aggressive and full of himself! As soon as I returned to Toronto, I sold the few shares I had for a good profit. As the months went by, the shares appreciated steadily and I always had this feeling that maybe I had made an error by selling. Not too many months later, the CEO was accused of illegally siphoning off about $600M from the company. We later learned about his unabashed, opulent spending of the monies he stole, including shelling out for $6,000 shower curtains, expensive artwork and lavish corporate parties. He was charged and convicted and served more than six years in jail until granted conditional release in 2014.

From $80B market capitalization to under $4B

Another example is **BlackBerry Limited**, formerly known as **Research in Motion Limited (RIM)**, a Canadian telecommunication and wireless equipment company best known as the developer of the BlackBerry brand of smartphones and tablets. While the early success of the company was undeniable, problems often develop when corporations have two co-CEOs. I find this to be a high-risk arrangement with a time bomb ticking. We may not know when the bomb will explode, but it will happen. While I have to admit that the RIM co-CEOs did a good job for many years, their arrangement and their relationship with the board ultimately led to strategic errors that caused the collapse of the company. Sales went from $20B in 2011 to about $3B by 2015. Most importantly, the company went from a market capitalization of over $80B to about $3B!

Preparation before promotion

Some things can only be learned through experience. You can't learn it at school and you can't get it by watching a video. You need to go through it. Wal-Mart entered the Canadian market in 1994 with the acquisition of 122 Canadian Woolco stores, at the time a troubled subsidiary of Woolworth Canada. Gradually, Wal-Mart renovated the stores and converted them to the Wal-Mart banner. All employees (+/– 16,000) were retained and got a welcome raise by joining the Wal-Mart family. A senior vice president of Woolco became CEO of Wal-Mart. Wal-Mart strategy for Canada was right on and has been successful for many years.

On the other hand, Wal-Mart's entry into Europe by attacking the German market first was not a success. Its entry in 1998 was short-lived; the company exited the German market in 2006 and sold its 85 Supercenters. Its 2006 expansion to Canada with Sam's Club was also poorly executed with the result that Wal-Mart closed its six SAM's Club stores in 2009. The moral of the story? Do your homework with modesty, listen to wise advice, simplify your approach and stay focused on doing the ABCs with excellence. And you will win. But if you cut corners, get arrogant and complicate your approach, you will lose.

Shareholders take a bumpy flight

Another example is Bombardier, a large multinational aerospace and transportation company in Canada that was founded back in 1942. This public company is controlled by the Beaudoin family, who has a controlling interest with special shares and a board of directors that includes many family members of the chairman, Laurent R. Beaudoin. While the chairman has a long list of honors and recognitions, you cannot have a public company and be controlled by a family. Stay private and do what you want, or go public and lose your privacy. It is always a red flag and a recipe for failure when I see companies with both arrangements. You ask for trouble when the board is composed of friends and family members. No matter how qualified they may be, they will be tempted to compromise their opinions and clarity of judgment by avoiding potential conflicts of views, ducking key issues and actions and staying away from "rocking the boat."

For a company founded in 1942 and with annual sales of $18B in 2015, Bombardier had almost $27B of liabilities and a negative equity of $4B. How do you get to these results after being in business for over 70 years? By complicating things.

Buy low sell high — easy to say, hard to do

Daimler-Benz, maker of the world-famous luxury car brand Mercedez-Benz, purchased Chrysler Corporation in 1998 for $36B. The new company, Daimler Chrysler AG, began trading on the Frankfurt and New York stock exchanges. The stock rose rapidly to over $100 per share. I owned a few shares at the time and was happy to see the shares appreciate in value. One day a business magazine reported how different the cultures of the two organizations were. The German culture was described as conservative, disciplined and structured, while the Chrysler culture was creative and full of risk-taking. At the time, the CEO of Chrysler was reported to earn many times what the new German boss made. While the acquisition looked great to deal makers, bankers and accountants, it did not look good to me. I sold my shares, happy and thankful for making an honest profit. It's not easy to sell shares when the name of the company is Mercedes. But as the months went by, more Chrysler executives were fired or left, and soon the profitability of Chrysler turned into losses. By 2003, Chrysler Corporation had cut over 25,000 jobs and was still losing money. Finally, in 2007, the Germans sold 80% of Chrysler to a venture capital firm for $7.4B and two years later paid to unload their remaining 20%. What a story — buy at $36 and sell at $7! But don't forget that for ten years, the patient was in intensive care.

This story reminds me of the saying "culture eats strategy for breakfast," a phrase originated by Peter Drucker and made famous by Mark Fields, president of Ford. It says that, regardless of its products, no company will flourish if the employees don't embrace a communal set of values and behaviors. Employee morale and engagement are key to company success. It is not only a matter of numbers, nuts and bolts, and strategies . . . culture, values, leadership and team spirit are the real keys to success.

Character is more important than talent and experience. Take it from me: more often than not, simplicity brings clarity, balance and wise decisions.

APPENDICES

1) Sales Pipeline
2) Sales Process
3) Weekly Sales Contacts
4) Monthly Sales Report
5) Yearly Sales Marketing Planner
6) KCPI Short Version
7) KCPI Long Version
8) Project Status Report
9) Task Status Template
10) Training Schedule Template
11) Sales Plan Template
12) KPI Template Sample
13) Sales Territory Worksheet

1) SALES PIPELINE

Name: Week Ending:

No.	Company	Location	Telephone	Contact	Position	Estimated Sales	R	Notes/ Comments
1								
2								
3								
4								
5								
6								
7								
8								
9								
10								
11								
12								
13								
14								

R = RATING **A** = close within 30 days **B** = close within 30 to 90 days **C** = undetermined close

2) SALES PROCESS

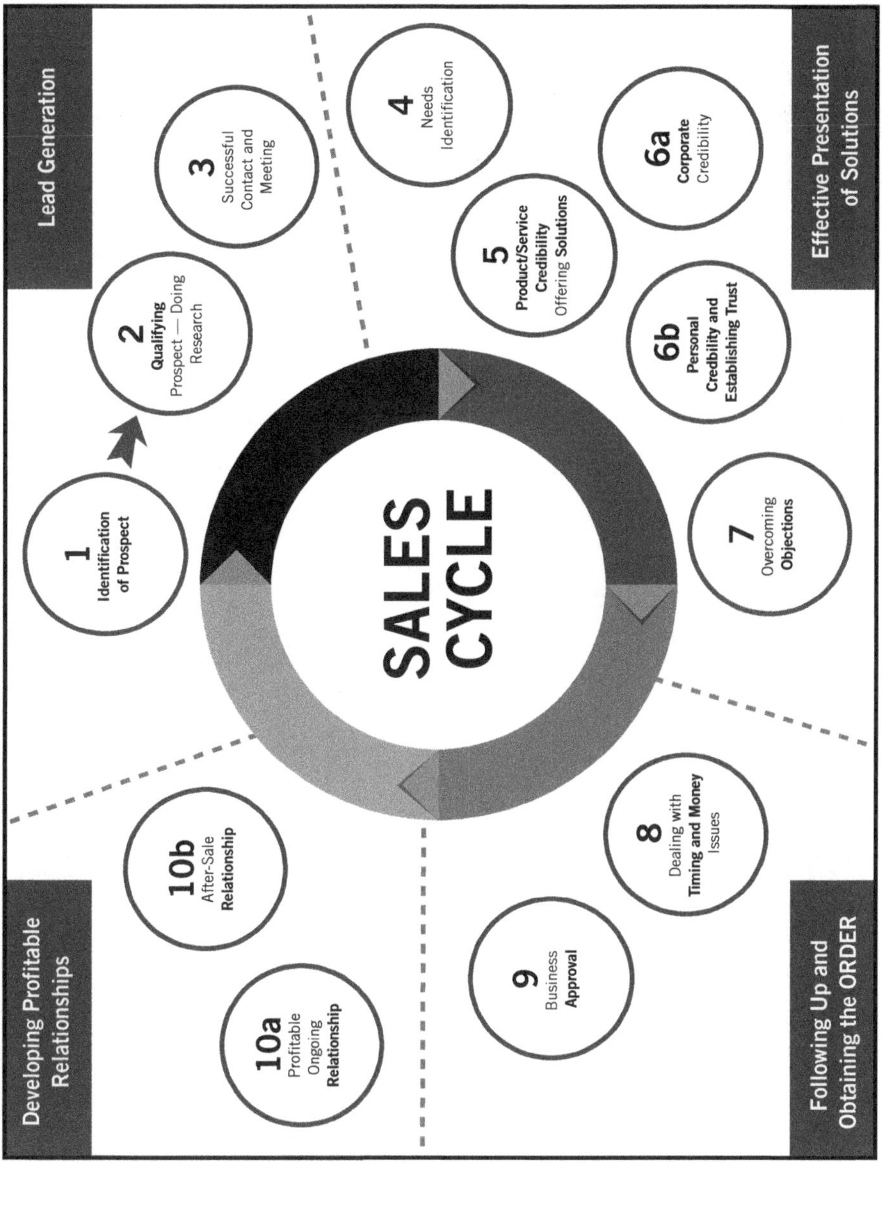

3) WEEKLY SALES CONTACTS

Name: ______________________ Week ending: ______________

	Company	Location	Telephone	Website	Contact 1	Position	Comments
1							
2							
3							
4							
5							
6							
7							
8							
9							
10							
11							
12							
13							
14							
15							

4) MONTHLY SALES REPORT

Name: ______________________ Month of: ______________

1) **Sales:**

Month $ ________ Budget Month $ ________ Sales YTD $ ________ Target YTD $ ________

Notes: ______________________________

2) **Presentations to Prospects** (P) and **Customers** (C) made during the month

	Company	Location	Name	Position	Telephone	Notes/Comments (Specify P or C)
1						
2						
3						
4						
5						
6						
7						
8						

3) **MARKET FEEDBACK** (Market needs, competitive intelligence, competitors, pricing, new products/services, research and development, associations, trade shows, etc.)

____

____

____

4) **FORECAST**

Month	Forecasted Sales	Objective	Notes / Comments
Month of	$	$	
Month of	$	$	
Month of	$	$	

Name: ______________________ Signed: ______________________

Date: ______________________ Manager: ______________________

5) YEARLY SALES MARKETING PLANNER

Month	Event	Focus	Media Used	Results & Notes	Other
December	Hanukkah, Christmas, Boxing Day				
Q4					
January	Let it snow, let it snow . . . Snowbirds time, Australian Open (Tennis)				
February	Family Day, Valentine's Day, Winter Olympics				
March	Easter, Spring is in the air!				
Q1					
April	Spring is here! Earth Day, Secretary Day, Masters (Golf)				
May	Soccer fever, Mother's Day, Labor Day, Kentucky Derby (Horse Racing), WEFA (Soccer)				
June	Summer is here! Camping, Father's Day, U.S. Opens (Golf), Wimbledon (Tennis), Stanley Cup (Hockey)				
Q2					
July	Canada Day, Independence Day (U.S.), Wimbledon (Tennis), FIFA World Cup (Soccer), British Open (Golf)				
August	Friendship Day, Holidays, PGA (Golf), U.S. Open (Tennis)				
September	Back to School, Yom Kippur, Rosh Hashanah, U.S. Open (Tennis), Summer Olympics				
Q3					
October	Thanksgiving (Canada), World Series (Baseball), Falling leaves				
November	Thanksgiving (U.S.), Remembrance/Veterans Day, Black Friday				
December	Hanukkah, Christmas, Boxing Day				
YEAR					

5) YEARLY SALES MARKETING PLANNER cont.

Month	Event	Focus	Media Used	Results & Notes	Other
December					
Q4					
January					
February					
March					
Q1					
April					
May					
June					
Q2					
July					
August					
September					
Q3					
October					
November					
December					
YEAR					

6) **KCPI (Key • Customer • Prospect • Information)** SHORT VERSION

COMPANY NAME

Other Trade Styles/Divisions

Full Address ______________________________

Telephone ____________ Fax ____________ www. ____________

Subsidiary of/Part of the Group of:
(When applicable give details on the parent company or the group)

____

____

Company Activity/Line of Business:

____

____

KEY PERSONNEL

(List all contacts including decision makers, users, technical persons, assistants, etc.)

	Name	Position	Tel./Email	Notes
1				
2				
3				
4				
5				
6				

Comments: (Specify: date and type of contact, personal, telephone, name & position of person contacted, brief summary of discussion, next steps — when, by whom)

____

____

____

____

____

6) **KCPI** SHORT VERSION cont.

Identified Needs:

Pricing:

Facilities Visit and Comments:

Customer Profile:

Our Product Line of Interest:

Specific Considerations:

Engineering:

What are the objective/concerns of the customer?

❑ Speed of service ❑ Turnaround time ❑ Price competitive ❑ Quality

❑ Range of products ❑ Growth of business ❑ Service ❑ Delivery ❑ Flexibility

❑ Frequency of change/alterations

Our Competition: price, volume, type, service, location, weaknesses

---

Referrals:

Notes:

---

7) KCPI (Key • Customer • Prospect • Information) LONG VERSION

COMPANY NAME

Other Trade Styles/Divisions

Full Address ______________________

Telephone ____________ Fax ____________ www. ____________

Subsidiary of/Part of the Group of:

(When applicable give details on the parent company or the group)

____

____

Part of the Group of:

____

____

Other Divisions & Subsidiaries:

____

____

Name of Salesperson/Account Executive:

Business Telephone: ____________ Business Fax: ____________

Home Telephone: ____________ Home Fax: ____________

Email Address: ______________________

Name of Manager:

Business Telephone: ____________ Business Fax: ____________

Home Telephone: ____________ Home Fax: ____________

Email Address: ______________________

7) **KCPI** LONG VERSION cont.

KEY PERSONNEL

(List all contacts including decision makers, users, technical persons, assistants, etc.)

	Name	Position	Tel./Email	Notes
1				
2				
3				
4				
5				
6				
7				
8				
9				
10				
11				
12				

D	Decision Maker	**Level of support**	
U	User	**H**	High
T	Technical Person	**M**	Medium
C	Coach	**L**	Low
E	Economic Person ($)	**P**	Problematic

Notes:

Organization:

(Draw a quick organization chart showing where key personnel are)

7) **KCPI** LONG VERSION cont.

Information on Key Personnel:

Provide information on each decision maker. E.g., Bill Smith is the decision maker. As senior VP he is interested in the economics of the deal. Has been in this position since 1992. Previously with ABC Company Ltd. Likes our company and is a good supporter of our products & services. Does not discuss price much, concentrates on service details. Likes to be informed of what is going on. Frequency of contact is about once every two months. Delegates day to day to John Doe, VP operations, and relies on Susan Grade for technical info. He reports to Alexander Great, the president. Bill is married with two children. Enjoys golf and reads history books. Enjoys Italian food.

___

___

Company Profile:

Describe industry, activities, annual sales, employees, profitability, etc. (attach D&B report, Equifax report, articles from newspapers and trade publications, customer internal documents, website info, etc.)

___

___

Key Strategic Environment, Business Trend, Marketplace, Their Competition:

Describe the strategy of this business and comment on their trend of sales and profits. Are they winning, losing or just holding their own? What are the major challenges the company is facing? Who are their competitors and how are they doing? Add any other information that would help us better understand this business and its market place. List important changes that have or are about to happen.

___

___

Need(s) Analysis and Level of Satisfaction:

Identify and list the main needs of this company. List those needs that are presently satisfied by our company and identify potential areas of needs for additional business. Address short term and long term. Please comment on the level of satisfaction and how good of a job we are doing. Give details as need be and attach any pertinent supportive information.

___

___

___

7) **KCPI** LONG VERSION cont.

Our Competition:

What is our competition and how are they doing? How/what/where/when/how much/why, etc., is the customer actually using our competition? Give details and estimate dollar and volume of business going to the competition. If the customer is not using the competition, explain the reasons and indicate if this situation can change. Indicate timing and estimate the likelihood of the change. Explain what is being done to improve our market share. List any actions we need to undertake. Attach any information you believe relevant.

Our Business: (History if a customer, projections if prospect)

List sales volumes, quantities, products, services, etc. Give comparable numbers whenever appropriate. Are we winning or losing? Is our business going up, staying flat or down? What are we doing to improve?

	Year 1	**Year 2**	**Year 3**	**Year 4**	**Year 5**
P1					
P2					
P3					
P4					
P5					
Total					

Comments:

Current Yearly Plan:

Provide yearly plan and milestones for Q1, Q2, Q3, Q4. List dollars and volume, assignments, jobs, etc., as need be. Also list pertinent events, meetings, annual reviews, etc.

7) **KCPI** LONG VERSION cont.

Information on Key Personnel:

Describe our business plan with this key customer/prospect. Identify strengths and weaknesses, investments needed, level of services, products, etc., for the next three years. List the things that have to happen for our plan to work. Include sales projections, volumes, profitability, etc., as need be. Include dates and any relevant milestones.

Historical Data:

Record visits, important meetings, entertainment events and costs whenever appropriate and applicable.

Engineering Section:

Record visits, important meetings, common projects, specific engineering challenges, suggested solutions, etc., as appropriate and applicable.

Credit and Collection Section:

	Name	Telephone	Email	Notes
A/P 1st Contact				
A/P 2nd Contact				
Comptroller				
Financial Manager				

7) **KCPI** LONG VERSION cont.

Credit and Collection Section:

	20XX	20XX	20XX	20XX	20XX	Notes
Credit Limit						
Highest Owing						
Terms						
Payment						
B2B CHEX Rating						
DNB Rating						

Notes:

Terms:
N30 (Net 30 Days)
N45 (Net 45 Days)
50N30, 50N60 (50% 30 Days, 50% 60 Days)
1%10N30 (1% 10 Days, Net 30 Days)
Special Terms

Payment:

PPT	Prompt
Disc	Discount
Slow	Followed number of days

Other Information:

Prepared/Reviewed By: ______________________ Date: ______________

8) PROJECT STATUS REPORT

Project Name	Client Name	Project Manager	Prepared By

	Activity	% Complete	Issues	Delivery Date	Owner	Notes
1						
2						
3						
4						
5						
6						
7						
8						
9						
10						
11						
12						

Status Summary:

8) PROJECT STATUS REPORT cont.

Budget Overview

	ITEM	Owner	On Track?	Notes
1				
2				
3				
4				
5				
6				
7				
8				
9				
10				
11				
12				

Company name ______________ Web ______________ Tel. ______________

Logo

9) TASK STATUS TEMPLATE

TASK	DESCRIPTION	ASSIGNED TO	STATUS	PROGRESS	NOTES
1				10% 25% 50% 75% 100%	
2				10% 25% 50% 75% 100%	
3				10% 25% 50% 75% 100%	
4				10% 25% 50% 75% 100%	
5				10% 25% 50% 75% 100%	
6				10% 25% 50% 75% 100%	
7				10% 25% 50% 75% 100%	
8				10% 25% 50% 75% 100%	
9				10% 25% 50% 75% 100%	
10				10% 25% 50% 75% 100%	
11				10% 25% 50% 75% 100%	
12				10% 25% 50% 75% 100%	
13				10% 25% 50% 75% 100%	
14				10% 25% 50% 75% 100%	
15				10% 25% 50% 75% 100%	

STATUS:

- ❑ VERIFIED
- ❑ COMPLETED
- ❑ IN PROGRESS
- ❑ CREATED
- ❑ DRAFT
- ❑ CANCELLED

10) TRAINING SCHEDULE TEMPLATE

TRAINING SCHEDULE	
For	
Position	
Starting Date	

Training Performance — Productivity & Quality

MAIN RESPONSIBILITIES
a) Copy main points or reduced version from job description
OR
b) Reference is made to enclosed job description

WEEK 1

W1A General Orientation: Employee manual, office tour, office routines, working hours, introduce to team members, telephone numbers, logistics, important contacts, workstation, stationery, storage, facilities, etc.

Covered with ______________________ on ________________________ ❑ OK

W1B Position Tasks:

Task 1 ______________ covered by ______________ on ______________ ❑ OK

Task 2 ______________ covered by ______________ on ______________ ❑ OK

Task 3 ______________ covered by ______________ on ______________ ❑ OK

Task 4 ______________ covered by ______________ on ______________ ❑ OK

Task 5 ______________ covered by ______________ on ______________ ❑ OK

Task 6 ______________ covered by ______________ on ______________ ❑ OK

Task 7 ______________ covered by ______________ on ______________ ❑ OK

Task 8 ______________ covered by ______________ on ______________ ❑ OK

10) **TRAINING SCHEDULE TEMPLATE** cont.

WEEK 1

Other Tasks

W1C Report Writing/Forms:

Report/Form 1 ____________ covered by ____________ on ______________ ❑ OK

Report/Form 2 ____________ covered by ____________ on ______________ ❑ OK

Report/Form 3 ____________ covered by ____________ on ______________ ❑ OK

Report/Form 4 ____________ covered by ____________ on ______________ ❑ OK

Report/Form 5 ____________ covered by ____________ on ______________ ❑ OK

W1D Mid-Week Review/Comments:

____

____

____

Covered with ______________________ on ______________________ ❑ OK

W1E Friday Review/Comments:

____

____

____

Covered with ______________________ on ______________________ ❑ OK

W1F

1) **Meet with General Manager:** Cover company history, mission, vision, capabilities, clients served, market, competition, team guidelines/principles, etc. This meeting should preferably take place during the first week.

❑ OK Meeting Date ______________

2) **Meet with Operations/Product Development Director:** Cover product line, client needs, design, product development cycle, product categories, outsourcing benefits and challenges, quality controls, service excellence, vendors screening, partnerships, alliances, etc. This meeting should preferably take place during the first week.

❑ OK Meeting Date ______________

10) **TRAINING SCHEDULE TEMPLATE** cont.

WEEK 2

Ongoing coaching by ______________ and assisted by ______________,

______________ and ______________ ❑ OK

Areas/Work Covered (Summary)

____

WEEK 3

Ongoing coaching by ______________ and assisted by ______________,

______________ and ______________ ❑ OK

Areas/Work Covered (Summary)

____

WEEK 4

Ongoing coaching by ______________ and assisted by ______________,

______________ and ______________ ❑ OK

Areas/Work Covered (Summary)

____

30-DAY REVIEW

Done by ______________ on ______________ ❑ OK

Briefly describe training and work covered during first 30 days. Quick evaluation of period.
Note employee feedback.

____

____

60-DAY REVIEW

Done by ______________ on ______________ ❑ OK

Briefly describe training and work covered during first 30 days. Quick evaluation of period.
Note employee feedback.

____

____

11) SALES PLAN TEMPLATE

Yearly Budget

Year ________ Territory ______________________ Salesperson ______________________

Manager ____ Date ________________

YEAR	January	February	March	Q1	April	May	June	Q2
This Year								
Budget								
Last Year								
YTD This Year								
YTD Budget								
YTD Last Year								

	July	August	September	Q3	October	November	December	Q4
This Year								
Budget								
Last Year								
YTD This Year								
YTD Budget								
YTD Last Year								

11) **SALES PLAN TEMPLATE** cont.

Summary of Top Customers Plan (Canada)

	Customer	Year	Year	Year	TARGET	Q1	Q2	Q3	Q4	
1										
2										
3										
4										
5										
	Subtotal									
6										
7										
8										
9										
10										
	Subtotal									

11) **SALES PLAN TEMPLATE** cont.

Summary of Top Customers Plan (USA)

	Customer	Year	Year	Year	TARGET	Q1	Q2	Q3	Q4	
1										
2										
3										
4										
5										
	Subtotal									
6										
7										
8										
9										
10										
	Subtotal									

11) **SALES PLAN TEMPLATE** cont.

Sales Plan (Year)

	Q1	Q2	Q3	Q4	Notes
Advertising and Promotions					
Calls					
Trade Shows and Customer Events					
Pricing					
Emails, Direct Mail, Newsletters, Social Media					
Other					
Other					
Date Reviewed	Date:	Date:	Date:	Date:	

12)

KPI TEMPLATE SAMPLE

KPI Template	Curr. Mth	Sample MLY	Diff.	%Sales	BM	YTD Act.	%Sales	YTD LY	%Sales	Diff.	B YTD	Comments
Sales 1												
Sales 2												
Sales 3												
Total Sales												
Dir. Cost 1												
Dir. Cost 2												
Dir. Cost 3												
Total COGS												
GROSS PROFIT												
Salary & Wages												
Sales & Mktg												
Admin/Office												
Facilities												
Other 1												
Other 2												
Overhead Subtotal												

12)

KPI TEMPLATE SAMPLE cont.

KPI Template	Curr. Mth	Sample MLY	Diff.	%Sales	BM	YTD Act.	%Sales	YTD LY	%Sales	Diff.	B YTD	Comments
EBITDA												
EBITDA%												
Interest												
Taxes												
Amort/Dep.												
Subtotal												
Net Profit												
Profit Margin												
Inventory												
Accts Rec.												
Av. Coll. Period												
FTE												
Op/Plant FTE												
FTE Other												
Production Meas.												
Quality Meas.												
New Customers												
Forecast		F%		FM1		FM2		FM3		FM4		
Other												
FTE Full-time Equivalent												

FM1 Forward Month 1 – 2 – 3 – 4

13) SALES TERRITORY WORKSHEET

Analysis and Yearly Plan

Salesperson ______________ Started ___________ In position since _________

Territory ____

History	Sales	Increase	%	Number of Customers	Trend	Notes
Year						
Year						
Year						
Year						
Year						

Top Twelve Customers

	Key Customers	Location	Sales	% of Total	Notes
1					
2					
3					
4					
5					
6					
7					
8					
9					
10					
11					
12					

Comments: Indicate direction of business (UP, STEADY, DOWN) and overall trend, is the relationship strengthening or deteriorating, competitive situation, market share estimation, potential future business, obstacles for growth, major changes, key remarks, etc.

Remarks/Notes: Cover new initiatives, new promotions, new sales tactics, sales strategies, key events etc.

13) SALES TERRITORY WORKSHEET cont.

New Business

	Key Prospects	Location	Notes
1			
2			
3			
4			
5			
6			
7			
8			
9			
10			
11			
12			

Comments: Indicate potential and existing competition, special needs, key people, key actions that we need to implement, obstacles and objections, estimate sales cycle, etc.

13) **SALES TERRITORY WORKSHEET** cont.

Annual Sales objective YEAR 1 No. of customers ____________

Annual Sales objective YEAR 2 No. of customers ____________

Annual Sales objective YEAR 3 No. of customers ____________

Quarter	Sales	Comments
Q1		
Q2		
Q3		
Q4		

Comments: Indicate in the comments section the main actions for the quarter (e.g. special promotions, discounts, trade show participation, advertising, etc.)

Overall Mix	Repeat Business	New Business
Business Mix in %	%	%

Sales Person Remuneration	
Monthly Target	$
Quarterly Target	$
Yearly Target	$
Tactical and/or strategic objectives	

Explain any special strategic or tactical objectives for the year (e.g. secure the ABC account, introduce our new service to 30% of the customers, have 40% of customers use the new internet ordering system, etc.)

Comments: General comments about the territory: expense report due date, sales report due date, sales leads notes, expected visits per day and per week, complaints handling, customers events, trade show attendance, forecast requirements training issues and programs, team play, etc.

____

____

Manager ____________ Salesperson ____________ Date ____________

Next Review ____________ Mid-Year Review ____________

Last Quarter Review ____________

BIBLIOGRAPHY

Chemers, Martin. *An Integrative Theory of Leadership*. Mahwah, NJ: Lawrence Erlbaum Associates, 1997.

Churchill, Neil C., and Lewis, Virginia L. "The Five Stages of Small Business Growth." *Hbr.org*. May 1983. https://hbr.org/1983/05the-five-stages-of-small-business-growth.

Dixon, Guy. "Avis overcomes reservations with purchase of Zipcar." *Globe and Mail.* January 2, 2013. http://www.theglobeandmail.com/globe-investor/avis-overcomes-reservations-with-purchase-of-zipcar/article6841893.

Grant Thornton LLP. "Private Company Succession Planning: Where Do You Stand?" *Grantthornton.ca.* 2011. http://www.grantthornton.ca/resources/insights/reports/Private_Company_Sucession_Planning_Where_do_you_stand_2011.pdf.

Gronstedt, Anders. *The Customer Century: Lessons from World Class Companies in Integrated Communications.* New York: Routledge, 2000.

Hansen, Sue. "7 Stages of Business Growth Review." *Suehansenspeaks.com.* Accessed April 23, 2015. http://www.suehansenspeaks.com/business/stages.htm.

Interbrand. Accessed June 10, 2015. http://www.bestglobalbrands.com/2014/ranking2.

Rumball, Donald. "The Six Stages of Growth in Ontario's Leading Growth Firms." *Ontario.ca.* March 2013, http://www.ontario.ca/document/six-stages-growth-ontarios-leading-growth-firms.

Wharton University of Pennsylvania. "Declining Employee Loyalty: A Casualty of the New Workplace." May 9, 2012. http://knowledge.wharton.upenn.edu/article/declining-employee-loyalty-a-casualty-of-the-new-workplace.

Acknowledgements

Many thanks to the many gifted people who helped me make *Maverick Leadership* a reality, starting with Priya who first gave me the idea and then encouraged me throughout the process. Priya always retained her smile while editing my long-winded sentences and kept her cool at all times. She was patient, effective and kept me focused. Thanks are also due to Jerry who has project-managed the book from A to Z and provided me with great advice. Many thanks are also due to Tania, Jennifer and Troy who have helped with all the design, typesetting, editing, proof reading and production behind the scenes. A very special thanks to Adam, Amber and Min at the best UPS store in Canada for their attentive service and for going beyond the call of duty so many times. Last but not least my deep gratitude goes to the entire Latif team with Ehsan, Elisa, Dirk and Daniel cheering lovingly from the sidelines.

Dedication

I dedicate this book to all my clients who have helped teach me the ins and outs of consulting while I was working for them and with them; to my ex-bosses, the good ones and the not-so-good ones who also taught me the ins and outs of management and; to you, the reader, for choosing *Maverick Leadership*.